A Few Special
Ghosts
I have met

I hope you believe in ghosts because then you will enjoy reading of the author's journeys, led first by Lily Cove and then others in search of solutions to the puzzling mysteries of what happened many years ago.

Ghosts are people from the past coming back to the present time to ask our help to make a change for them – very often to put something back which we have inadvertently disturbed.

Although they alert us to their presence in fantastic ways, they have all been friendly and I have been able to serve or help each of them in some way.

I hope you enjoy reading their amazing stories.

Lily Cove – a famous and tragic parachutist

Mary Queen of Scots – a tragic Queen

Sir Walter Scott – the Scottish historian

Lady Elizabeth Seton – a concerned mother

Cedric and Cecil – twin brothers in Cape Town

Author   **Neil Burns**   **1999**

Published by JocknDoris Publishers 1999

Prose Text © Neil Burns 1999

All rights reserved. No part of this publication may be reproduced, stored in a retrieval system, or transmitted, in any form or by any means, electronic, mechanical, photocopying, recording or otherwise, without the prior permission of JocknDoris Publishers.

ISBN 0 9535748 0 6

Printed in England by
The Amadeus Press Ltd., Huddersfield
Typesettting by
Highlight Type Bureau Ltd., Bradford

for

JocknDoris Publishers
Upper Moor End, Mamble
Worcs DY14 9JD

Original photographs by John Pitt, Stourport-on-Severn

Dedications
Dedicated to Jock and Doris, two faithful cats who inspired the name of the publishing company and to two other cats called Dot and Carry-one who kept me company whilst I wrote each chapter.

Acknowledgements
Tributes are paid to everybody who assisted in the compilation of this book, especially those in and around Haworth who have been so friendly and helpful. To name a few: Leonard and Elaine Ogden, Alex and David Southeran and of course Sharon Wright reporter for the Keighley News. But most of all to Lily Cove herself who guided me in my search for the solution to the mystery and who insisted that I publish this book to make people aware of what actually happened on that fateful day 11th June 1906.

Chapter Index

Page		Host
4	Lily Cove	Lily Cove
7	Old Injuries	Lily Cove
10	Off to Haworth	Lily Cove
12	The White Lion	Lily Cove
15	Parachutists	Lily Cove
19	Molly Sedgwick	Lily Cove
20	Pinkie Castle	Lady Seton
23	The Scarf	Lady Seton
25	Back to Bewdley	Lily Cove
28	Waiting for the day	Lily Cove
30	Back to Haworth	Lily Cove
33	In the crook of my arm	Lily Cove
36	Exploring with Lily	Lily Cove
39	The Cemetery	Lily Cove
41	Ponden Reservoir	Lily Cove
45	Droitwich Spa	Lily Cove
49	My first job	Cedric and Cecil
52	Getting Advice	Cedric and Cecil
55	Nether Kineddar	Sir Walter Scott
59	Whisky	Sir Walter Scott
61	The Old Man in the Road	Sir Walter Scott
63	The Story is not yet over	Lily Cove
64	Mary Queen of Scots	Mary Queen of Scots
67	Linlithgow Palace	Mary Queen of Scots
72	Reims	Mary Queen of Scots
78	Flight of fancy	Mary Queen of Scots
82	Three Cornered Hat	Lily Cove
88	Meeting Lily	Lily Cove
93	Wrapping it up	Lily Cove

1.
Lily Cove

I first met Lily Cove when I travelled up in 1992 to Halifax in West Yorkshire England to carry out an audit, and over the last five years we have become close friends despite the fact that she died in a parachuting accident in 1906.

"Who on earth was Lily Cove?" did I hear you say?.

Well, she was a wonderful young woman who made a name for herself by being a daredevil parachutist in the days before aeroplanes were invented. She used to travel the country with Captain Bidmead and his amazing hot air balloon and would take off into the air in a harness strapped below the balloon.

She was a happy go lucky twenty year old from London who realised that she would have exciting adventures far from the big city if she followed the intrepid Captain Bidmead.

She loved the company of young men and was seen on occasions to join them after a hard days work in some light refreshment.

She was fearless and wore outrageous clothes for her time, being seen in bloomers or frilly long knickers which she wore under her skirt and which she discarded just before she took off into the air. When the balloon reached 1,000 feet or so she would pull a lever and detach herself from the balloon, descending gracefully but quite quickly to the ground.

People would come from near and far to see her exploits, and usually she would be carried shoulder high, back to her quarters by a cheering crowd. Her exploits were so daring that questions were asked in Parliament. Should a young lady be allowed to do something so dangerous? Surely a law ought to be passed to prevent it?

I knew nothing about any of this in 1992 when I first travelled up to Haworth in West Yorkshire.

I am a Scots Chartered Accountant, 56 years old and live near Kidderminster in the West Midlands of England which is over 180 miles south of Haworth. People say I don't look like a Chartered Accountant which I take as a compliment.

Like Lily, I thoroughly enjoy life and look forward to each new day to see what fresh excitements and challenges it will bring.

I have a small group of accounting clients that I like to think I give a personal service in looking after their financial and tax affairs.

I have one particular client who runs a successful business in Stourport in Worcestershire and he asked me to produce a set of accounts for a subsidiary company of his in Halifax.

Being a Scots Chartered Accountant I insisted on going to visit the company to carry out a proper audit on site, and so I asked the Directors to book me a hotel and make all the arrangements.

The man I went there to meet was - I was to discover - a wonderful character called Leonard Ogden, truly a salt of the earth. He is a few years older than me, with rugged good looks and that earthy accent from West Yorkshire which is so distinctive. He ran a company called Double O Engineering because his surname was Ogden and his partner's was Oddy and what could be more appropriate than Double O?

When I set off in my car I was in a buoyant mood looking forward to my trip to deepest Yorkshire and the first part of the journey went smoothly as the car was running well - at its happiest zooming along the motorways. However as I left the motorway just short of Leeds under that beautiful sweeping bridge down into Halifax, I had a strange feeling of excitement mingled with fear, as if something strange was going to happen.

2.
Old Injuries

I often get these feelings and they always turn out to be portents of something shortly to happen, but they are never clear enough to give me any real clue as to what that might be.

In other words, during an ordinary office day, I might in the middle of the afternoon start to feel grumpy for no reason at all. Then later I find that my car has a puncture or some minor thing has happened to annoy me . This should be useful to me but I never know with enough accuracy what is wrong or what is going to happen, so that I can never under normal circumstances do something about it.

But I knew as soon as I turned off to Halifax that it was not going to be an ordinary trip.   I first started having strange pains in my right foot so much so that I could not hold the accelerator down, and after trying with my left foot I realised that it was not at all practical and in fact very dangerous.

Whatever was wrong?   I felt the pain in the ball of my right foot which began to throb in a very particular spot exactly where I had a very painful veruca removed when I was still at school - maybe forty years ago!   I stopped half way into Halifax to confirm directions and was surprised that I had taken completely the wrong turning, and the woman behind the counter said "You don't look very well at all".

I forget what I bought, but as she passed it to me, she remarked "that's a very nasty scar you've got there" and the mark I have where I accidentally drove a chisel into my left hand close to my thumb was bright red - livid almost as if it hadn't yet healed.   But that had happened more than forty years ago!

With that I felt an itch on my side and without thinking scratched quite vigorously at the spot, only to feel terrible pain and can remember my mother saying to me "leave that alone, Neil!"   It was the site of the scar I was left with after a very bad bout of shingles when I was fourteen or fifteen years old - again some forty years ago. Why, in the world of goodness, were all these old injuries springing into life all of a sudden?

I knew the answer well. Something was going to happen to cause me considerable distress and that it would be from the past a long way back, would be my best guess.

I had arranged to meet Leonard at the foot of the hill at a pub called the Calder & Hebble and he was there bang on time. He led me directly to the factory in Halifax where we arrived early in the afternoon. There was no pressure to meet deadlines which meant lots of time to do the work required.

I was of course worried that my distress was going to come from meeting my new clients and checking their books. Had there possibly been some fraud - that, I may say, had seemed an unlikely occurrence, from what I knew of the staff so far - or was I going to unearth that the company insolvent?

The factory or engineering workshop was set in an old disused woollen mill, typical of the "dark satanic mills" which punctuate the landscape of the early industrial revolution around these parts. It had six or eight storeys of symmetrical but beautifully proportioned windows many of which were now broken. The engineering works was in the below ground floor and I had to descend three or four large steps which were worn away by time, so that unless your feet travelled exactly the same path as those before you, you might well stumble.

I struggled because my foot was still hurting me considerably, so much so that I was hobbling and felt positively embarrassed about it. I called out and a huge man - a sort of gentle giant - came towards me and he told me where I could find the gaffer who turned out to be Leonard, the most charming, down to earth man you could wish to meet.

The factory had six or eight engineering lathes and turners and they were making parts for the more complicated label printing machines which I had seen being put together in Stourport near Kidderminster. As soon as went down the stairs, I felt very welcome and I was amazed that I felt no pain at all in any of the strange places I had experience it previously. Surely the welcome alone and relaxation couldn't just have that effect?

The books were in good shape and every test I did gave me the positive result which I was expecting. It was a near perfect audit so much so that Leonard was a little disappointed that I had not found anything wrong. Perhaps there was something of the feeling you might get at the dentist - having eaten sweets and chocolates all year - when you are told that no fillings are needed. Has the dentist looked carefully enough?

But no the books were great and I remember asking whether they were absorbing enough overheads to pay their way and when I suggested that they really ought to increase their prices a bit my shares really went up!

I remember having pleasant coffee and about half past four or so we were all done and almost at a loose end. I asked if I could look at the rest of the building, which turned out to be six floors of sad emptiness. Leonard took me on a guided tour and it was amazing to see the vast areas of workspace where many hundreds of people must have worked, now vacant and dusty and dirty. Again a slice of the past. I asked Leonard "When was the mill closed?" "some forty years ago" he replied.

But there was no distress here only fond old memories and my foot was not even slightly sore and as we headed back to the car Leonard said "I've booked you into an old Hotel in Haworth which I think you will like, but its quite a way off, near my home in Keighley in fact."

"That's wonderful", I said "Let me follow you and we can take both cars and I can set off direct from the hotel in the morning".

"Good plan", we all agreed.

3.
Off to Haworth

Yorkshire - or parts of it - can be very hilly and Leonard, I think, had chosen the hilliest parts on his route. I was glad I had a powerful car because trying to keep up with him on these very steep climbs and hairpin bends took some doing. He knew the road of course like the back of his hand and was testing the driving capabilities of his new Accountant.

It struck me that I couldn't even remotely have handled it with my painful foot but as we went higher I rather enjoyed the double de-clutching at corners to keep me within sight of Leonard.

It seemed like 15 miles as we travelled up hill and down dale seeing all sorts of extraordinary sights including giant windmills of the modern type, harnessing power but rather spoiling the landscape.

Soon I saw signs which said Bronte Museum or Bronte Parsonage and I am ashamed to say that I did not at first know that were entering Bronte Country.

Haworth is of course a major tourist attraction as it was the home of the Bronte family and the sisters Emily and Charlotte had lived with their father at the vicarage and had written their great novels there.

We went up a near vertical hill to get round to the top of Haworth and Leonard seemed headed for the hotel car park which we found, after having to steer rather gingerly between some of the late visitors and tourists who crowd into every possible inch of the small village.

Leonard went straight ahead in the car park and, in a very gentlemanly gesture, took the furthest left hand most near a path which ran up to the Bronte Museum, leaving a nice gap for me to fill in right beside him.

I drove up towards the gap and the pain in my foot struck me like a touched nerve in a tooth, so much so that I simply could not park there.

By this time Leanord was out of his car and I re-set myself to try again. But try as I could, I was not happy parking in that spot. Every way I attempted it, I was uncomfortable and I said rather sheepishly to Leonard, "I am awfully sorry but I would rather park over there."

"Please yourself" he said rather politely because it was a little discourteous of me, to say the least, not to take the spot he had chosen for me.

As I settled some 50 yards away Leonard came over and I apologised, saying, "I just couldn't park there." He looked puzzled and said "Whatever is the matter?".

Together we went across to the spot and there in the grass just close to where the bonnet of the car would have been was a very large stone which looked completely out of place.

I thought first that it had fallen off the nearby wall which ran up to the Museum but it was too big for that and also the wrong shape and yet this stone worried me.

As I went closer I felt worse and worse and it was clear to me that this was the cause of my distress - but why ever should I be affected by a stone which looked quite ordinary in all respects?

Leonard was looking at me oddly so I said "Let's get the suitcase" and I set off with him towards The Old White Lion hotel which is just round the corner. The Hotel stands right at the top of the famous steep hill commanding the best position and you couldn't miss it if you tried. We walked down the cobbled roadway which is really now only used by tourists to the splendid old hotel.

"How clever of you to get me in here" I said to Leonard, who beamed from ear to ear. "I am so pleased - I thought you would like it. We know them quite well here", was his reply.

4.
The White Lion

I felt an amazing warmth as I approached the hotel, to a welcome far in excess of what a stranger would normally receive.   I was meant to come here and I was excited but apprehensive at the same time.

"We've been expecting you", said the receptionist who was called Sarah. "Mr Ogden said you would be coming. We've given you room five as we thought you wouldn't like number seven."

This seemed a strange remark to make to me, but as she took me up the stairs I was immediately engulfed in the atmosphere of the place, which was so warm encompassing and friendly.

Sarah opened the door for me and I put my suitcase straight on to the bed which is unusual for me because normally I only unpack in the morning - if you understand me.

"Thanks very much Sarah", I said and followed her down to the front hall again where Leonard was chatting to some friends. "I'll go and fetch Elaine now and we'll be back about eight, if that's OK", he said.

"Wonderful. -   I shall be very happy here", I said   "You were very clever to find this hotel for me."

I walked up and down the stairs and along the corridors just because it made me feel elated just to do so.

There were any number of articles of furniture in the corridors and in the corners of each nook and cranny, which were all panelled in dark wood which looked a hundred years old or more.

My room looked out on to the tiny square at the top of the hill with a window that swung out and it had a long wispy net curtain which threatened to head off through the window with the wind.

I couldn't explain why but I just felt happy oh so happy.

RAC LICENSED RESTAURANT   **AA** B.H.R.C.A. MEMBER

OLD WHITE LION HOTEL

Haworth, Keighley, West Yorkshire BD22 8DU Tel : Haworth (0535) 642313 Fax : (0535) 646222

MR N Burns

Room No: 7

Reg VAT No: 406 0129 01

Date	1992	June 10									
Brought forward											
B&B	30	50									
Inc Terms											
Lunch											
Aft. Tea											
Dinner	59	~5									
Tea/Coff											
Wines											
Bar	3	88									
F/Food											
Cigs.											
Service											
Tel.											
Paid Out											
Papers											
Deposit											
Sub Tot											
V.A.T.											
TOTAL	93	83									

SERVICE CHARGE NOT INCLUDED : LEFT TO CUSTOMERS DISCRETION

Proprietor: Mr. J. K. Bradford

I went down and spoke to Sarah who was an amazing girl. She had a slightly lazy eye and most uneven teeth but as you looked at her face she became quite beautiful, warm and attractive. She was the sort of girl that you know would be wonderful to kiss, but unfortunately I didn't get the chance.

I knew the moment I came into the hotel that it was haunted.

All my prickles were up and my head itched and I knew we were in ghost country!. Friendly ghost country but why, oh why, had I had the dreadful and somewhat embarrassing business with the stone?.

It would be a long time before I discovered why.

Leonard arrived with his wife Elaine and his daughter Julie and we went through and ordered what promised to be a delicious dinner in the dining room, which again had attractive dark wood panelling.

We had a beautifully relaxed meal with Leonard and his party and all enjoyed the good food and surroundings. Elaine was a match for Leonard in every way being a real Yorkshire character with a warm face. You could see as well that Julie was their daughter as she seemed to inherit a little from each of them.

We spoke a lot to the waitresses about the hotel but because I didn't want to upset Leonard I didn't mention anything about feeling that the Hotel was haunted.

Later I chatted to Sarah on reception about whether the hotel was in fact haunted, and she said "We don't really accept that it is but of course some people say so!"

And then she told me the long story of Lily Cove who was the remarkable girl of 20 who travelled the country with Captain Bidmead and his hot air balloon, and who became a famous parachutist.

5.
Parachutists

Remember in 1906 there were virtually no aeroplanes and so the sight of a hot air balloon was in itself remarkable.

For weeks ahead posters would go up stating that Captain Bidmead was coming on a certain day and for the cost of sixpence you could go to the Gala field and see the balloon being filled. It was tethered to the ground of course as it was filled up and only allowed to rise a few feet - just enough to enable Lily and sometimes Captain Bidmead to attach themselves to a special harness and cross bar for Miss Lily Cove to sit on.

Miss Lily Cove was famed for her beauty although she was sometimes accused of being too forward and even coquettish. She was only 20 years old and came from London but not much else was known about her. She was tall and elegant and usually wore a long flowing dress in a darkish material with underneath long dark knickers which came to below her knees, tied with provocative bows.

These caused an uproar as when she went aloft in the balloon she discarded her skirt as it would interfere with her descent. Many said of course it was so that all the assembled gathering could see her shapely, long legs - perish the thought - it shouldn't be allowed. She had a beautifully narrow waist and usually wore a waistcoat which accentuated her fine figure.

Amid great drama and ceremony Captain Bidmead would check Lily's harness and the balloon, then check she was ready and then to a great cheer from the crowd, he would release the strong rope holding the balloon which would start its ascent very slowly, ensuring that the spectators below could see Lily for as long as possible.

The field was always set at a good vantage point obviously fairly high but near a village to gather the biggest possible crowd. Once Lily had reached about 1,000 feet she would wave to the assembled watchers and then pull a lever to release herself so she descended to the ground, helped only by a very primitive parachute made of wood and canvas which served merely to slow down her descent.

She had little or no control over where she landed and tales are told of landing on roof tops and in trees. If Captain Bidmead had done his calculations correctly, then Lily would land close to the field to be surrounded by a cheering throng of well-wishers, who would help her to her feet and cheer her all the way back to the village.

However, on the 11th of June 1906 things did not go according to plan.

The balloon was supposed to go up on the Saturday but difficulties were apparently encountered in getting the balloon inflated sufficiently, and the launch had to postponed to the Sunday afternoon.

Stories written about it and remembered accounts of it all vary and I was to discover months later much more of the truth, but what there is no doubt about is that Lily landed a long way from the field. Many say she was out of sight of the crowd having gone behind a hill for some considerable time.

When Mr Charlie Merrall reached her at the farm, she was motionless, lying on the ground next to her parachute, not 50 yards from the edge of Ponden reservoir and all the efforts of the villagers could not restore her to life. A special cart was set up and used to rush her prone body back to Captain Bidmead who was distraught with grief.

What should have been a wonderful cheering crowd celebrating her return ,turned into a miserable group of people crying their eyes out at the sight of this beautiful young girl, who had been killed under such mysterious circumstances.

"Lily spent the night before the tragedy here" said Sarah "in room seven!" "That's why we didn't put you in room seven because she often appears to guests - particularly if they are sensitive to ghosts - and we could tell immediately you came in that you were aware of that".

I went to bed with my head buzzing with the amazing and tragic story and I had difficulty sleeping, not because I was frightened at seeing a ghost but because I had an strong feeling that I must meet Lily and help her in some way.

How frustrating that I was in the wrong room!

I left a small light on during the night as that is a welcoming sign and I slept well and heard no noises or anything unusual, but that was probably because I was hoping that I would.

I woke at 7.30am with the alarm call that Sarah had arranged for me and got up ready for another day.

The room had not enough space for a bath so a shower was the order of the day, and not being used to showers I remembered too late that the water might be too hot as I went in and I burnt my foot as I stuck it in to test the temperature of the water. I tell that only because I want to give the reader all the facts, as a good story teller ought.

6.
Molly Sedgwick

Shortly after my first trip to Haworth, I got in contact with Molly Sedgwick who was the wonderful lady mentioned to me by the people at the Visitors Centre in Haworth. She had written a book about her mother Dolly Shepherd who was a famous parachutist at exactly the same time as Lily was at the height of her fame.

Dolly had only recently died at the age of 97 so it was just remotely possible that she had met Lily Cove and they were probably friends as well as rivals. If only I had met her mother before she died, I might have learnt about Lily at first hand.

I spoke at length on the telephone to her daughter, Molly and she was kind enough to send me a copy of her book which highlighted how incredibly dangerous the parachuting was.

One story told of how two of the girls went up together in the balloon. One girl's harness became entangled before they jumped and was thus virtually useless so her friend managed to move, hand over hand, until she reached her and they jumped together holding each other for grim life and somehow both landed without injury.

Other stories tell of up-currents and parachutes therefore going up rather than down and of parachutists never being seen again.

Add these dangers to the obvious ones and you cannot overstate the risks that those pioneers faced.

7.
Pinkie Castle

I was a boarder at school at the famous Loretto School in Musselburgh, just outside Edinburgh, and one term I was a prefect in the House which was situated in Pinkie Castle. This contains the famous Painted Gallery, a room big enough to sleep 16 boys which had a ceiling beautifully painted by some unknown artist which captured the imagination as one lay in bed looking up at it.

I was lucky enough, however, to have my bed in 'Rest and Be Thankful' an amazing turret room only big enough for two which I shared with a tough 17 year old called Beamy Smith - so called because he was a big lad and played front row in the rugby team.

This was a boy's public school. There were no girls at all. So it was a great surprise to me when, after lights out one evening early in the term, we saw the door to 'Rest and Be Thankful' open gently and a tall, very feminine, slender figure in a long dress glide across to the window.

We were on the third floor and to get there you had to negotiate at least two rather tricky spiral staircases and it was right at the top corner of the Castle. The window itself was very small and, as I remember it, the wall of the turret was round so at best you would struggle to see very much out of the window.

But our guest was quite sure what she wanted to do and she moved about, constantly trying to get the best position to see out of the window.

She was clearly frustrated as she could make no progress and she seemed in distress because her face showed a frown, not of hostility but of grief.

Who was this wonderful person because she was not a member of our school!!

I lay in awe and considerable fear because this had to be a ghost I would have said but - then again maybe not - so I decided to say nothing and wait a while.

Pinkie Castle

Two or three days passed and again it happened. This time she arrived silently at the door and went across to the window to peer out into the dark ,and then after ten minutes or so she would shrug her shoulders and return to the door with a look back as if to say I'll try again another time.

This time I noticed that it was not only a clear night but there was a strong moon.   I couldn't remember if the conditions were the same the last time we saw her.

Then I wondered if Beamy had seen her too because maybe he was fast asleep.

"Are you awake?", I whispered

"Yes", was the courageous reply. "I couldn't possibly sleep if the Lady of the Tower was here".

"Did you see her?", I asked.

"Of course I did!- I was frightened that maybe you hadn't"

Whatever does she want and how could we help her?

We decided, Beamy and I, that if we opened the window we might allow her to see more but we were worried that she might jump out the window, until we realised that the window was so small that she couldn't possibly get through.

We waited for nearly two weeks before we saw her again, but we had the window open every night - nearly freezing to death in the process. But she did come back and this time she looked right out the window, and took off a headscarf which she had round her hair and cast it out of the window as if in the hope of catching something.

This was repeated time and again over the next few weeks, until we realised that the school term was nearly over.   Our friend was less frustrated but clearly still very unhappy.

One night, right at the end of term, she threw her scarf so vigorously out of the window that she lost it.   Both of us noticed that she left without it about her head.

8.
The Scarf

This made Beamy and I very excited because maybe we could find her scarf and return it to her.

The following morning we were both up with the larks and decided that an early morning run was called for.

We set off round the castle but it wasn't as straightforward as you might imagine, because there was a very high wall running one side which effectively split the castle surrounds in two.

One side was open to the windows of the Painted Gallery and the other to the windows of the Headmaster and his rooms!!.

Beamy and I, however, were determined and we sneaked round to the wall right under our turret window. We could not believe what we saw. There was the very same scarf. It had got caught in the old ivy which climbed up the wall.

It was possibly ten feet up and we jumped and leapt as if we were in the lineout at rugby but we couldn't reach it so Beamy said "Come on Neil I'll lift you up" and he hoiked me up so that I was fully six feet off the ground.

I could just about reach the Scarf and after five or six tantalising misses I caught it but as I did so we both heard the dreaded Headmaster roar, "Smith come here!" and Smith did just that and left me stranded, hanging on to the ivy.

I leapt outwards into the space Beamy had left clinging on to that wonderful scarf at the same time. "What the devil are you two doing out here at this time?", roared our dear Headmaster.

Well, our lips were sealed and as we were marched to the Headmaster's study a glance between us said that nothing on earth would make us talk.

Thank goodness the Head had not seen the scarf which I had tucked under my jersey and Beamy very sportingly went in first to be caned.

Four sharp cuts later he came out of the Head's study grabbing from me the scarf which I passed to him. I don't think I even felt the four strokes I got, so keen was I to get back to Beamy and examine the scarf.

We only had that mystical scarf for one day because, that same night our Lady returned and found it where we had left it for her at the window.

She put it on and instead of walking straight to the door, she went to Beamy's bed and then mine to give us both a kiss on the forehead to say 'thankyou'. I can still feel the warmth of those lips and the texture of that scarf to this day.

"What were you chaps beaten for this morning?" asked everyone and we just said "Oh nothing really".

The reader may care to note that the ghost of Pinkie is well documented and apparently in 1760 Lady Elizabeth Seton of the house had a baby out of wedlock and in distress and confusion took it to the Turret and threw the little baby out of the tiny window to an accomplice outside.

She couldn't see properly and must have had the agony of not knowing whether her baby had been caught safely.

Had she thrown her scarf for us to find and demonstrate that there was no baby there?

We saw her a few more times later that term but on these occasions she was smiling - a little knowing smile, suggesting to us that she knew at last that her baby was fit and well - and that at least was something.

It was long phonecall to Sharon in Keighley and my story had whet her appetite. "We will see you in Haworth on the tenth and I will bring a photographer." she said.

9.

Back to Bewdley

I came down to breakfast at the White Lion, and was greeted by a new receptionist called Judith, who was young and attractive and wearing the mandatory black miniskirt that waitresses seem to have to wear. She had a neat figure and wore the clothes well.

We immediately got talking and I noticed for the first time that there was a plaque on the wall, carved in wood showing Lily in her harness sitting below the huge balloon.

It stated that on 11th June 1906 Miss Lily Cove was tragically killed in a mysterious accident over the Gala Field at Haworth. Fondly remembered by Captain Bidmead, Charles Merrall, and many others who saw the tragedy occur.

"Did you see anything last night Mr Burns?" asked Judith.

"No I didn't - but I didn't really expect to." I replied   "I must come back and stay the night in room seven on the anniversary of the night that Lily slept here because she has left me messages loud and clear that I must be of service to her."

I knew this with absolute certainty and so I got Judith to book me in for 10th June which was another four months away.

After a wonderful Yorkshire breakfast I went up to my room and in the corridor passed a tall girl dressed in a long black skirt, who gave me a little dipped curtsey and a friendly but demure smile.

"Good morning" I said

"Good morning sir - Shall we see you again?" she asked

"Yes indeed" I replied

Little did I realise then that I would see her many more times over the next few years.

I paid my bill and double checked that my room was booked for June 10th. I was keen to explore a little more of the hotel and asked Judith if there were any cellars or dungeons and she took me to the back where the beer was dropped into the cellar.

"Here is where the alterations were done" she said and explained that a stairway had been changed which practically barred the entire old passageway out at the back.

There was strange narrow stairway which was blocked by a modern freezer. And then a modern archway in the converted garage downstairs leading to a flat at the back to a door with 'Private' in bold letters on it.

"We never go in there" said Sarah

Now those of you who know ghosts will realise that, very often, they have been disturbed or made unhappy by somebody changing the way things were, by, say, altering or removing a staircase that they used to use.

The very reason for them coming back to haunt their resting place is to try and persuade the present occupiers to restore things to their original state so that the ghost could resume his or her old ways.

This was particularly true of Sir Walter Scott who met the author in Saline in Scotland as explained in Chapter 19, which the technically minded might wish to read before proceeding.

The journey back went quickly; at one point I was overtaken by an identical white BMW to mine who which had the number plate NKB 1. Now my initials are NB and so it intrigued me. But I couldn't overtake to see the driver.

Then a most remarkable thing occurred.

I received a call from a client Maurice Cohen who was concerned about a number of business matters and we talked on the phone for some time. I was in the car travelling down from Halifax and he was in his office in Kidderminster some hundred miles or more away.

The car phones in those days had a facility whereby messages could be recorded 'back at base' if you chose to do so. You could then dial in later and request a playback of the message left for you. So in our office nearly

200 miles away there was a tape recorder linked to the phone. What quirk of electronic wizardry caused it to happen I will never know, but the entire conversation which we had between my car and Maurice Cohen was recorded on the office tape recorder which I was sure was not connected in any way.

The only possible explanation was that I had checked in to see if there were messages for me at the office and while I was doing that Maurice phoned me and the crossed line clicked the recording to start.

There is no way in this world you could set up that set of circumstances but I can assure you that it happened, and was only one of many strange unexplained phenomena which occurred between my visit to Halifax and my return visit to Haworth on 10th June.

10.
Waiting for the day

The months passed very slowly as I was keen to go back to see Lily but I had to wait till the actual day, 10th June, the day before the anniversary of her death.

I was keen, however, that there should be someone there to record anything which might happen, so I wrote a letter to the local paper asking them to put an ad in the paper along the lines.

"WOULD ANYONE WHO HAS SEEN THE GHOST OF MISS LILY COVE OR IS INTERESTED IN SOLVING THE MYSTERY SURROUNDING HER ACCIDENT IN 1906 PLEASE CONTACT NEIL BURNS C/O P O BOX 112 at KEIGHLEY NEWS"

My intention was not only to publicly state that I was coming but also alert Lily to the fact also.

The reaction was amazing.

A young lady called Sharon Wright, who was a reporter with the paper, rang me almost the next day to say that she had seen my letter and would like to meet me.

I said I would be delighted and she asked me for some background to my ghost hunting activities, and I told her on the phone about having met Sir Walter Scott (Page 55) and my love affair with Mary Queen of Scots (Page 64), although my first real meeting with a ghost was in Pinkie Castle in Scotland (Page 20).

After my phone call Sharon put a full page in the paper as shown on the next page.

I think all ghosts are friendly. They are merely trying to contact someone to help them do something they cannot do for themselves, rather like children in a way.

They are asking for help, very often, to put something back the way it was or to correct a wrong or a misunderstanding.

After a chat with Sir Walter Scott, a woman who threw her baby off a castle and a dead South African boss, you'd think any civilised ghost-hunter would be happy to rest on his laurels, but seemingly not. After speaking to the still-earthly SHARON WRIGHT (not a ghost writer, we can assure you), a spectre-chaser from Kidderminster is still convinced a dead lady parachutist wants to talk to him in Haworth. Oh, and he still wants a word with Mary, Queen of Scots...

WILL THE GHOST OF LEAPING LILY REVEAL ALL NEXT WEEK?

A spook-spotter from Kidderminster is re-visiting Haworth next week in the hope of meeting a troubled ghost and solving an 86-year-old mystery.

Mr Neil Burns is convinced the ghost of parachutist Lily Cove, who died mysteriously in a terrible accident on Haworth moor in 1906, is trying to contact him.

He plans to stay in the same room occupied by Lily on the eve of her death – June 10.

Mr Burns has met many phantoms in his life, most notably Sir Walter Scott who appeared to him for a chat in Scotland to sort out a controversy over some papers.

Mr Burns, 49, who has a computer business in Kidderminster, is not perturbed at the number of ghosts who seek his acquaintance. He enjoys ethereal encounters and has high hopes of one day tracking down his heroine Mary Queen of Scots.

Now he is planning an unearthly rendezvous with Lily in the Haworth hotel he believes she haunts to find the truth of what happened on the fateful day she died aged just 21.

Lily was famous in her day as a liberated lady parachutist, quite unabashed by showing her legs as she floated skywards attached to a hot air balloon. She toured the country with manager Captain Bidmead pulling great crowds with her spectacular leaps.

She arrived for Haworth Gala in June 1906 and locals travelled from miles around to witness the feat. The first jump was postponed because of bad weather, but rather than disappoint her public, Lily decided to stay overnight in the Old White Lion Hotel and try again the next day.

She climbed into her balloon, drifted up to Ponden Reservoir and made her much-rehearsed jump. But to the horror of the crowd and the consternation of the Captain, Lily became detached from her chute and plunged to her death.

A horse and cart was sent from Haworth to collect her body. Later, after a ceremony in the hotel, she was buried in the cemetery overlooking the route of her last flight.

HAWORTH PARACHUTE ACCIDENT 1906

● The story of Lily's luckless leap is told briefly on this postcard, available in Haworth, which succinctly sums up the entire tragedy in a few lines on the reverse. Pictured are Lily, the luckless Captain Bidmead, whom Mr Burns thinks may also contact him, hot-air balloon complete with attached parachute and attached Lily, and the gravestone which marks the lady's final resting place. Spooky possibilities or not, Lily's legend is another talking point for the tourists.

Nobody ever discovered why her chute failed and her death caused a furore in Parliament leading to moves to ban women from dangerous stunts.

The mystery remains and now Mr Burns thinks Lily wants to tell him something. He describes a series of strange events from the first time he visited Haworth to see a client and had trouble parking his car.

Beset by strange sensations he had to move his car several times before he could park. He remarked to his companion that there was something very odd there.

They went back to the Old White Lion for a drink but on entering, Mr Burns says: "I experienced shivers down my spine and I knew straight away that it was haunted because this has happened to me before."

He discovered Lily had slept at the hotel the night before she was killed and is determined to return to sleep in the same room on the anniversary of her stay.

He says: "Ghosts have a purpose in appearing. They are troubled by something but they never appear just to frighten people. They want to find out something or change something."

He had more hair-on-end feelings in the cellar of the hotel. Now he says: "I think she wants to be able to tell me that it wasn't her fault, or tell me what happened. Or maybe she wants in some way to pass the blame on."

On Valentine's Day he sent her a good luck card. It was left open in the room for her to read. He says: "I am sure we are going to get a sign or a signal."

Mr Burns later found a two of spades on a friend's toilet floor. This is very significant, he insists. It means Lily will materialise and there will be some digging involved, either literally or metaphorically, before the end of the saga.

He is also investigating a village stone which gave him peculiar vibes in the car park.

Mr Burns claims he has been seeing ghosts since boyhood. The first appeared to him on a school trip in a Scottish castle. It was of a woman who appeared to stare in anguish from where she had hurled her baby long ago.

Then there was the deceased owner of the firm he worked for in South Africa.

Often, when working late, an old chap would visit him for a chat. Mentioning it to a colleague he was casually told it was the dead ex-owner.

"The trick," he confides, "is to be relaxed. They will only appear if you are open to them."

Hotel manager Mr Keith Bradford is more sceptical and refuses to comment on the ghost-hunter's planned adventure.

● Anyone who has seen Lily or has information on her can contact Mr Burns on 0562 742137.

11.
Back to Haworth

I set off for Haworth on the 10th of June, just after lunch and the car seemed to be coasting on air as we flew north. I was excited but apprehensive as well as there had been extensive publicity in the local paper following my talk with Sharon Wright and my advertisement.

As I travelled, however, I noticed that the scar on my left hand started to flame up as did the old scar on the side of my tummy, but surprisingly no pain at all in my foot - which had of course been the main problem the last time I came up. Did this mean anything?

It obviously made it easier for me to drive, which if Lily was the cause was good news because she clearly wanted me to get there.

As I cut off from the motorway another strange thing happened. I had suffered - again when I was at school - with a blocked saliva gland which for no reason at all used to block just under my tongue and again become quite painful, so much so that it stopped me talking.

Sure enough, nearly 40 years since it had first troubled me it flared up again and when I stopped at a chemist to get some TCP, I had to point to it on the shelf and the staff just took me for an old codger who couldn't speak very well. A swill in TCP cleared the trouble and I think the message from Lily was quite transparent. "I want you to come, but don't say too much!"

I followed the winding, narrow roads across the moors, which in itself is a wonderful experience - free as anything with wide open spaces all around you and always a breeze to clear the air and your head.

I stopped just before Haworth to survey the scene and to make a plan. I got out of the car a looked back across the dales where Lily must have floated on that day exactly 86 years ago.

I filled out my chest, broadened my shoulders and felt good - confident and convinced that I was here to do some good. I parked in the same car park as before but a full ten cars space away from the dreadful stone and without going to see it I strode to the ticket dispenser to purchase a ticket. It was only after I had paid for it that I realised it was not necessary, as parking was free after six in the evening and it was exactly seven o'clock. I got my case from the car and strode down to the cobbles and straight on to the hotel.

I checked in with Sarah who greeted me with great excitement saying "Everyone seems to know you are coming".

"That's good", I replied, as that was what I wanted.

"Does Lily know I'm here?", I asked.

"I am sure she does", said Sarah.

I went up the warm corridors and stairs, following Sarah who opened up room seven for me with a key that turned both ways - if you know what I mean. It seemed just as easy to open the door clockwise as anticlockwise. The lock simply slid back either way.

The room was a little smaller than I had expected but very welcoming and again I laid my suitcase on the bed.

"Lily got your card", said Sarah.

"How did you know it was from me?" I asked.

"Because she opened it", and there by the side of the bed was a card with the envelope lying beside it with the Kidderminster postmark. "Just to make you welcome it is", Sarah added.

I just had time to wash and freshen up before the phone rang to say Leonard and Elaine were downstairs. They were pleased to see me as I was to see them and we went to the little bar for a drink first.

We were tense and excited at once, wishing the time would pass quickly but equally wanting to savour the moment. We talked about all sorts of things particularly the stir that the article in the paper had caused.

"Some people say you shouldn't mess with things", said Elaine and Sarah, when she was serving us, said "The owner of the hotel is not very happy really as he doesn't like the publicity."

Later we had dinner in a corner booth which was the nicest spot in the dining room, but strangely I felt restricted and had some difficulty breathing and - most unusual for me - I twice had to pop outside for a breath of air.

All the talk was about Lily and what it must have been like 86 years ago. She must have been tense, knowing that the next day she was going up in the balloon. We wondered where Captain Bidmead must have stayed and whether it was also in this hotel.

After dinner I took Leonard on a short guided tour with Sarah's help and when we went down stairs to the spot where they had changed the staircase. I realised that the old staircase must have come though the corner booth in which we had sat for dinner.

Of course! That explained the breathlessness, in that somebody was making the point that we shouldn't be there. They wanted the air and the space for themselves.

Leonard and Elaine didn't want to leave and kept asking me, "will you see Lily tonight?" and I kept saying, "of course I don't know but I am almost certain she wants to see me."

I went to bed at a quarter past midnight which was late for me and I slept with the little bathroom light on, so that there was just a glimmer of light in the room.

I slept soundly with a postcard of Lily in my right hand as a welcoming sign.

12.
In the crook of my arm

We have two wonderful cats at home called Jock n Doris who are great friends but quite different. Jock is a large strong black tom and Doris a small fluffy tortoiseshell lady.

Often when I go to sleep at home, if I happen to be a bit tense, Jock seems to sense this and hops on to the bed and sleeps in the crook of my right arm. It's turned into a ritual and once he is comfortable and has settled down then he is set for the rest of the night.

So when I woke in room seven and noticed that something was in the crook of my right arm I was not surprised at all. The bed was pushed down and there sat Lily, in her long dark skirt, right at my side and she had wriggled in to the spot so favoured by Jock.

She was beautiful and I recognised her immediately from the photographs I had seen of her on postcards and in the paper, and of course this was the girl I had seen in the corridor the last time I was here!!

She was wearing a long dark skirt, as before, with a waistcoat above it and I could see her face which had delicate soft features and a friendly mouth, moist eyes and above all, thick lustrous black hair. She seemed tall but maybe that was because I was looking up at her.

"I am glad you have come", she said.

"So am I and I am pleased to meet you", said I.

"I have waited many years for you to come", said Lily.

Without moving, because I didn't want to disturb anything - just as if Jock had been there, I started talking gently to her.

"Why me?" I asked and all she would say was, "Because you fit with all the pieces and you've been to Droitwich - wait and see - you will soon find out".

"What do want me to do for you?", I asked.   "First you must move my stone. - It is in the wrong place", she replied. "Where must I put it?", I asked.

And again she just smiled as if to say - "I will show you."

"There are lots of people who think awful things of me and poor Mr Merrall. I was a good girl despite what people say", said Lily.

As I chatted to Lily I became aware of a lovely feeling of warmth and calm as if under a spell and I was captured by it completely.

Lily told me she had just left the rest of her party who were in another room at the far end of the hotel, past the stairway which had now been changed, and through the door marked 'Private'.

Captain Bidmead was there with his rather grand moustache and of course Charles Merrall, who's father was the owner of the local mill and one of the leaders of the local community, so at twenty-two he was already a wealthy and important man.

Lily then told me of their plans for the next day.

"Charles and I are in love, and tomorrow we are going to elope but his family would never accept me as his wife. We thought if we eloped in front of everybody that would show that we were serious."

It was obvious this was true - just to look at Lily's eyes when she talked of him you could see the sparkle of happiness there.

Lily carried on, "Charles has been wonderful and, of course, a perfect gentleman and we want it all to be exciting so we plan this daring escape"

"I have been with Capt Bidmead for two whole years and he has told me that I am the best balloonist he has ever had. When I told him I had fallen for Charles Merrall and wanted to elope with him he understood and agreed to let me go on certain conditions .

"First we have to find a replacement parachutist who must be just as able and daring and of course who could fit into the special clothes which have been specially made for me.

"Second we must arrange a spectacular handover and this is what we plan to do tomorrow."

"You see we have found a wonderful new girl called Elizabeth who is just the right figure and in fact had long dark hair just like me. We planned just before take-off for Elizabeth to take my place on the balloon. Then during the flight Charles and I are going to elope and the crowd will be far too engrossed in watching the balloon to see what we are up to."

"Then of course when the cart goes out to find the new girl Elizabeth, she will stand up and pronounce to the world that "I am the new Lily Cove" and it would be a spectacular start to her career."

I was about to give a warning to Lily when she said "There is nothing you can do today, Mr Burns, but watch and follow and I will help you find out exactly what happened. We will meet again like this in another place nearer your home."

I don't really remember any more because an all encompassing warmth came over me and I slept wonderfully well.

When Lily left I can't tell, but if it was at all like Jock then it would be at the last moment. When I woke - I can't be certain - I thought there was a wisp of wind and on the table by the card was a piece of white lace. It looked like a piece that would have been a collar but it still had to be sewn onto the dress.

I treasure that piece of lace because Lily gave it to me.

13.
Exploring with Lily

Whatever would today bring?

I knew Lily would lead me and so I had only to move forward and she would guide me.

I had a good breakfast and then met Sharon Wright and a photographer.

I made it very clear that I was not here to make a newspaper story, but to genuinely find out what I could do to help Lily and her memory and to do her a service.

Before going up to room seven to take the pictures that appeared the following day in the Keighley Times, I told them of chatting to Lily last night and how beautiful she was.

In the room they noticed the card and were amazed that this was casually on the bedside. I showed them the spot where Lily sat and told me to move the stone.

Another reporter called John Hewitt from the local Telegraph newspaper joined us and I explained that Lily would lead me during the day and they could follow if they wanted, but I would not be deflected from where Lily wanted to go.

We went first to the stone in the car park and whilst they could stand right beside it, I still had a horrible feeling coming from it.

I went up the path to the Bronte Museum and met Jane Sellars who gave me a reception that was courteous but somewhat cool.

I inferred that anything that drew attention away from the Brontes and their writings was unwelcome and that I should look elsewhere if I wanted to find anything more about Lily.

"What about the stone?" I asked. "What stone?. It's probably just rolled from the wall above". But we knew that wasn't true.

"How long has it been there?", I asked. "I don't know", was the answer (and "I don't care" was the message given by the shoulder shrug).

I was convinced that it had come from somewhere else although obviously some time ago.

"Go to the Visitors Centre - they will probably know", was her only advice.

We then trundled off to the Visitors Centre where we met three splendid ladies all of whom were keen to help us.

I was beginning to enjoy this and as we were waiting for the librarian to look up something for us, I was studying a beautiful blown-up photograph on the wall behind the counter.

It was apparently a famous photograph looking out over a windswept grassy dale way into the middle distance, a landscape from which, I understand, one of the Brontes had drawn some inspiration for their writing.

Out of sheer mischief I said to Sharon, "Was that a rabbit I saw!", and we all peered at the wall.

"There it is again!", I shouted and Sharon was so engrossed she only snapped out when someone shouted "it's only a photograph!" - and we all laughed.

Kathleen Cole was extremely helpful and wracked her brains to help us find the right field.   She thought that an old aunt of hers would remember and got her on the telephone.

"You must also see Ian Dewhurst - he is the local historian and knows everything."

The senior lady said that she was certain that the so-called Gala Field was now known as the Cricket Field.

One person told us that the balloon was filled using coal gas and a main two inch line had be used to produce enough gas.

Someone else said that they dug a long trench to the base of the balloon and covered it up so that when they lit a fire at the end of the trench the hot air ran along it and filled the balloon.

Never matter, there were any number of people keen to tell us about the day, although it was all from stories handed down.

We then met Arthur Hartley, who seemed a fund of knowledge and told us many of the stories about the happenings on that day so many years ago.

14.
The Cemetery

As we walked together, he said "you must visit Lily's grave in the cemetery," and for the first of many visits we walked up that hill to the local cemetery. An amazing place in a very exposed corner with the cemetery at a very steep slope so much so that it was an effort to climb up.

Lily's grave is the very first one you come to on the corner just to the right of the impressive entrance. As I went, with some trepidation, towards it, I read that it had been erected by public subscription some time after Lily's tragic death. On the headstone you could clearly see the balloon with Lily sitting below it and waving happily to the crowd.

The inscription showed the name:

Elizabeth Mary
(Miss Lily Cove)
Parachutist

There was tiny little garden of maybe six inches deep by two feet across where someone had planted some saxifrace which was obviously thriving. I went up round the headstone to see the back and in doing so I steadied myself against the slope by holding on to the headstone which to my amazement was so loose as to be in danger of falling over.

I steadied it - which was almost a balancing act in itself - and exclaimed that "this could fall at any moment", and as I did so a rabbit ran out from the base of the stone. Was that possibly the rabbit I saw in the picture at the Visitors Centre? Maybe I wasn't seeing things after all?

I looked at the base where the rabbit had come from and there was a very large hole which was, remarkably, the exact shape of the stone that had caused me so much grief in the car park. I was overjoyed at how clear the signal was! Lily wanted her stone back so that the headstone would be safe again.

IN
LOVING MEMORY
OF
ELIZABETH MARY,
(MISS LILY COVE,
PARACHUTIST,)
DAUGHTER OF
THOMAS CHARLES COVE
OF LONDON,
WHO DIED JUNE 11TH 1906,
AGED 21 YEARS.

I later wrote to the Convenor of the cemeteries in Bradford as you will see from the various copy letters and I am delighted to say that they did a splendid job in excavating the stone and replacing it at Lily's headstone.

"It fitted perfectly", said Mr Congreve when he told me about it, "but it was a major task to lift it and get it up to the cemetery - still it's a job well done." What an amazing thing.

Noone has ever been able to explain who took that stone because it was big and it was heavy. It would have taken a concerted effort by several men to lift it and a major effort to excavate it in the first place. Why had they taken and then apparently just dumped it, because apart from irritating me it served no purpose. We then took the car to go round the various reservoirs, because it was clear that water had been a contributory factor in all the mystery surrounding Lily's death.

15.
Ponden Reservoir

We set off first for Ponden Reservoir where everyone seemed convinced Lily's fateful landing took place.

I must explain that the roads round Haworth are a complicated maze of criss-cross and twisty roads, so it is very difficult to keep one's bearings and as many of the roads go down dales and then over hills it is extremely difficult to know where you are.

We spent two or maybe three hours following our noses, meeting people and it was amazing how many people said "We've been expecting you!".

The head gamekeeper and his wife had some tea and cakes ready for us almost as if we had an appointment. He told me his ghost story about the girl in black who used to arrive in a carriage with four horses, come into the house and change into a white dress and leave again in the same carriage.

As we sat having tea we all saw a carriage arrive and admired it. Then we saw the girl get out of the carriage in a long black dress with her head in a cowl almost as if she was hiding her face.

As she walked into the house she turned towards us and I immediately recognised Lily's smile and her warmth I recognised immediately. "She changes very quickly" said the gamekeeper as both Sharon and John Hewitt said, "We must go and speak to her", but when they got out to the gate there were only the tracks in the dust of the wheels of the carriage, as Lily was gone.

"You have set this up haven't you!" John Hewitt said to the gamekeeper, "We are from the Press - why didn't you tell us and we could have taken a photograph."

"Then Lily would never have come", was all he needed to say, "I have seen that carriage a hundred times and I don't know where it comes from and I don't know where it goes to, and I have never been able to touch it or get close enough top prove it's there.", he explained very patiently.

"But we saw it", said Sharon, "We saw it!"

I wondered why Lily had changed from black to white but I was sure it was a good sign. I thanked the gamekeeper's wife for tea and we were on our way.

How did I know to go there? Whatever possessed us to be on that road at that time if it wasn't with a little help from Lily?.

We wanted now to see where Lily had landed and the gamekeeper said, "I know exactly where that is", and gave us specific instructions which I can no longer recall, but we came round a corner to an extraordinary cottage which had a display of rats hanging up all across its front.

I wouldn't normally trouble the reader with this but it has stayed in my mind ever since. There were fifty rats - big ones all hung up across this cottage. For what purpose? It was eerie and thoroughly unfriendly but the lady there was pleasant and didn't seem at all put out by these blessed rats. Our gamekeeper had said "Don't be frightened of the rats", so we were on the right track.

We were shown the field where Lily is supposed to have landed and it was very close to the water. I knew exactly where to go, without any doubt, being drawn up the field towards a wall.

I had an urge to be beside Lily and so I lay down in the grass close to the wall quite a long way from the road.

As I lay I felt pinned. Have you ever had the really rather nice sensation of sinking into your mattress in bed so deeply that you feel you must be touching the floor?. Your back is so comfortable it is glued to the mattress and nothing can move it.

That is how I felt as I was lying there on the grass in my overcoat pinned to the ground and I had to ask Sharon to help me up. "Why did you chose that spot?" said the rat lady.

"I don't know of course" was my reply but I was not at all surprised to find out that that is exactly where they found Lily.

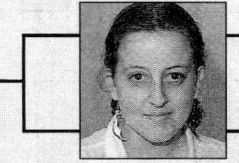

Memo from SHARON WRIGHT to all would-be reporters: what is the correct journalistic procedure when your interviewee becomes glued to the grass by supernatural suction? Answers on a postcard to NEIL BURNS, pictured right, spook-spotter extraordinaire.

LEAPING LILY AND THE SECRET OF THE STONE

'Did the daring damsel's ghostly bottom dent the bedspread?'

'Was this derring-do death really just the cover for a broken heart?'

JUST A MINUTE! I'M GETTING SOMETHING TO DO WITH STONE!

We KN reporters know how to rove, I reflected, as I stood up to my ankles in daisies, notepad in hand, a supernaturally-prone accountant lying at my feet communing with a corpse.

It is not every day you follow a suited chartered accountant up hill, down dale, over walls and across graves in search of a message from a long-dead lady parachutist.

No, last Thursday was not to be a day as other days as I went to meet Neil Burns, the 50-year-old Scottish accountant from Kidderminster visiting Haworth on the anniversary of the death of Lily Cove. He had come at her call, he said.

Lily, 21, died at Haworth gala on June 11, 1906 when her celebrated parachute jump from a balloon went horribly wrong and she fell to her death in a field near Ponden Reservoir.

Nobody knows why her much-rehearsed jump went awry, but I was to share many theories as I travailed through Haworth and surrounding windswept moorland following Mr Burns who was following Lily.

We began at the Old White Lion Hotel where Mr Burns admitted staff had been polite but determinedly shtum on the indelicate matter of dead people.

Soon KN photographer Julian Hodgson and myself were quipping and posing in Mr Burns' bedroom (the one where Lily got her last kip) and, purely for professional picture-taking purposes, I had to spend some time hiding in the bathroom.

Mr Burns told us how he had slept holding her picture and was quite sure he felt her sit on the end of his bed throughout the night.

It should be stated here that Mr Burns is the picture of respectability and has an endearing and charming manner. So even when he is telling you of the chats he has had with ghosts down the years, and how Lily Cove is calling him to Haworth from the spirit world, you are not as disturbed as you might otherwise be.

Julian departed and we set off on our strange journey. Mr Burns was convinced Lily had a task for him to do and that task had something to do with an unremarkable-looking rock in the car park near the Brontë parsonage.

Each time he went near it he reported feelings of distress and stiffness in his limbs. He said there was something Lily wanted doing with this stone – but what? And why?

Off to the parsonage museum where director Jane Fellars appeared. She was the first of many who greeted Mr Burns' eccentric inquiries with a poker face and a polite helpfulness. They know the beat of different drums, up Haworth way.

No, she knew of no reason why the rock was special. But she told us the car park was the site of the demolished Sunday School.

Farewell director, away to the house of Rachel Chaplin, 79, who Mr Burns had met earlier and thought might know something helpful.

She filled us in on some general history of the village then provided Mr Burns with some cuttings from her garden tub and we turned the corner to the information centre.

The ladies of Haworth information centre will never snub a fact-finding challenge, however bizarre. Mr Burns wanted to know exactly where Lily set off from on the day of the gala, 86 years ago.

So out came books, maps, postcards, leaflets. Assistant manager Kathleen Cole wracked her brain, then she wracked the brain of an old relative down the telephone, then she wracked the history-stuffed brain of local oracle Ian Dewhirst.

Eureka: he said it was the West Lane cricket field behind Haworth Methodist Chapel.

Ms Cole grabbed her cardy and offered to take us there, still not batting an eyelid.

Mr Burns was still confused about what Lily wanted and I was still trying to quell any ghost-discouraging cynical vibes I might be exuding.

Ms Cole hailed friends outside, and one, who adamantly wishes to remain nameless, said he would take us to the field and also to Lily's grave.

He looked scornful when the idea of driving was mooted.

En route Mr X recalled village gossip which had rumbled among locals after Lily's death. Some said she had had an ill-starred romance with a local mill owner and committed suicide.

So was her derring-do death a cover for a broken heart? He also explained the gala feat could well have been organised by one of the big mill families because they were forever trying to out-do one another.

We strode to the field and learned more interesting snippets from our forthcoming guide. Apparently the balloon which took Lily to her doom was filled not with hot air, but coal gas piped from the Haworth Gas Works over two or three days.

Still no sign from Lily, still no clear idea of the significance of the car-park stone. Then we went to see her grave and the gravestone carved with a balloon and paid for by public subscription.

And it was there that Mr Burns finally had his revelation. He gripped the headstone to try and focus better on Lily then exclaimed: "Dear God! It's loose! It could fall over at any time!"

Of course, he said, that was the message, that her gravestone was in peril and needed urgent repair. THAT was why she drew him to the Haworth stone, as a pointer to the problem.

He said: "It is obvious and clear. She's telling me that stone must be used to stop the gravestone falling over."

Well, if you say so, Mr Burns.

Mr X looked uncomfortable and said: "Aye, well, 'appen." Then he tried, as a building-trade man, to explain the rudiments of foundations, finance and repair to the thunder-struck Scot and how his plans were easier said than done.

Our companion gone and message received or not, we still had to see Ponden Reservoir and the nearby field where Lily had crashed to the ground to be found dying by local labourers and later her manager, the dashing Captain Bidmead.

We were guided to the spot by the obliging head keeper of the moors John Benson. And before taking his leave he shared his own ghost story with us. He told how he and his wife had seen a strange apparition at their isolated ex-coachhouse home in 1968.

Both had independently seen a crinolined lady emerging from a stage-coach helped by a top-hatted gentleman. Spine-tingling stuff.

And so to the field I mentioned at the start of this tale, the scene of the tragedy all those decades ago. An ordinary enough field, it seemed to me, and the owners were not at home.

I queried the wisdom of going in uninvited, but Mr Burns "felt" it was all right and soon my feet were engulfed in mud. I forebore from comment then and did similar minutes later when he felt a sudden compulsion to lie full-length on the ground with his eyes closed.

I stared nonchalantly across at the reservoir, straining for ambience.

Then he told me he felt inexplicably "magnetised" to the ground and would I help him up.

Always ready to do battle with strange forces, I obliged.

A popular theory surrounding the inexplicable death of Lily turns on her reputed terror of water. Some believe she thought she would land in the reservoir and detached herself from her parachute in unthinking terror to avoid drowning.

In the field Mr Burns said: "I can feel the fear she felt. But I feel that I have done most of what I was supposed to do. It was like someone she was pointing to, but I feel slightly disappointed now it's over."

Me too – undeniably I had a sneaking hope of seeing something likely to go bump in the night. A report of a ghostly bottom-imprint on a bedspread was hardly enough.

Mr Burns, it is known by Sir Walter Scott has not been above appearing to on occasion, speculated: "Maybe she didn't appear because in a way she didn't have to."

Well for this particular reporter, she had to. Still, whether or not Lily Cove lives on as a troubled ghost, her mystery remains.

An early woman pioneer, a fearless adventurer and crowd-puller extraordinaire, Lily, was undoubtably cut off in her prime. Why and how, we will probably never know.

"Most other people don't take the trouble to walk up the field", said she, "Are you a friend of Lily's?".

"I like to think so", I replied.   "It was the gamekeeper who told us about you"

"Gamekeeper?", she said   "Yes", I said.   "Well, if it's John Benson you're referring to, he died nearly 50 years ago but stories of the carriage are still told", said the rat lady.

I saw Sharon about to open her mouth to say, "But we just had tea with him", but she thought better of it!

Having wound our way back to Haworth, Sharon and John thanked me for a amazing day and I said, "you must thank Lily - she laid it on for you."

"Careful what you say in the paper because people don't always believe" was what I said.

"But we saw her!" said Sharon

Too true.

I made my way back to the cemetery as I wanted to be alone with Lily and I lay down again on top of her grave and had the same sensation as if I was being pinned and unable to get up.   I lay like that for many minutes.

Remember: the cemetery was on a distinct slope, so I was at an angle and could look our across the reservoir and the lakes.

What a wonderful spot to bury Lily and I was sure she would be at peace once her stone was replaced.

Later I returned to the car park and visited that stone and, do you know, it had no horrors for me at all.   It was at peace and it knew that it was soon to be returned to its proper place.

16.
Droitwich Spa

When I was travelling back to Kidderminster, it struck me that I had not asked Lily very much about Droitwich. Droitwich is a Spa town only ten miles from where I live and has been popular for two centuries as somewhere for the rich to travel to and take the waters. Droitwich Spa is how it is always referred to and the waters there are renowned for curing or helping all manner of ailments.

I had a client there who has become a good friend of mine so I scheduled in one of my quarterly visits so that I could maybe chat to them about Lily.

An ironmongers business has been in the same spot in the High Street of Droitwich for 90 years and parts of the shop are much older than that. The building is the old timber frame structure -black and white and oozing with character. The walls look as if they haven't had a coat of paint since then. This adds enormous charm to the place and I think is partly why it is so popular amongst the locals because it is part of the town.

"You will be able to get it at Machin's", is what you hear people say. Some of the stock I have counted must be twenty years old and they do have just about everything and will go to any length to find an item - or get it for you if it's not in stock or get it for you.

When I got there I worked for a good hour on the computer before Andrew Machin, the owner, came in.

We chatted about business, as usual and then he said " I must show you something - I was going through some old papers when you last called and look what I found".

It was a very old order book, so old that the edges of each page were dark brown as if age and decay had been eating away at the pages gradually from the outside in.

"That is amazing - it must have been used by...", "My grandfather" interrupted Andrew, "isn't that extraordinary!"

With that, he handed me the book and I opened it at random and the date on the order flew out at me - 11th June 1906 - the exact date of Lily's death!.

"There is something bizarre here", said Andrew, "because I have looked in that drawer many times before and have never noticed that book. But after speaking to you I just had to look again and open it up."

The order was for some parts for bicycles including handlebars to be sent to Rudge Whitworth in Yorkshire - not twenty miles from Haworth.

So I explained everything to Andrew who up until that point had no knowledge at all about Lily - let alone the date - and the coincidence was just too great to ignore. What was the connection between Droitwich and Haworth?

Andrew promised to look into it and said "I think we have relations in Yorkshire and that is where my grandfather came from."

So between us we started asking some questions about the company who had sent the order.

It seemed to be a company run by a distant relative of Andrew's whose name was Charles Kerler who now lived in Sheffield with his family. So I phoned them and they seemed very interested and suggested I travel up to see them.

In fact when I got there I spent almost the whole day with them and they insisted that I stay the night. They also mentioned that they had stayed at a fascinating little house in the middle of Worcester which was called "7 The Tything" a most unusual address. Worcester is only ten minutes away from Droitwich.

What made it all the more extraordinary was that I recognised that address particularly because the building had been re-developed amid some controversy by an Architect called Keith Backler who shared an office with me some years ago in Kidderminster.

The controversy surrounded some old fireplaces which were of historical interest and should have been preserved but were inadvertently lost in the restoration.

Order No. 25

CENTRAL HARDWARE STORES,
HIGH STREET,
DROITWICH, 11/6/1906

From H. R. MACHIN,
GENERAL & FURNISHING IRONMONGER, &c., &c.

Messrs Rudge Whitworth Ltd

Please supply as follows, quoting above number on Invoice:

1 – No 5 Speed Iron. – 22" Frame
26" Wheels. Aluminium Rims – 26 x 1½
Aero Special Tyres. 84 gear
Handlebars ¼ drop, similar to those marked rider in sketch enclosed. (Something between 72 & 86)
Otherwise to list Specification
1 – No 703 Lamp

Above is urgently wanted. If you cannot put on rail Thursday at latest please wire me, as my customer has to come in from the country, & does not want a lost journey.

Sundries ordered a week ago not to hand. If not dispatched, please send handle per return post, & remainder with above bike to oblige

H R Machin

There were so many threads here to pull together.

Had Lily wanted to come to Droitwich or had she been to Droitwich before because remember she came from London?. Maybe she had come up with Captain Bidmead to Droitwich or Worcester and wanted to return there?.

But how did I fit in? As the auditor of Andrew's Company there was a connection but a very tenuous one.

My own father was orphaned when he was thirteen and I was always told that his cousin lived in Longniddry but his photograph held a remarkable resemblance to Andrew Machin's father. They were both the same age and why had my father come down to Birmingham to be married?.

There was some definite link between my father's family and the Machin's. While I pondered, this Andrew's amazing old Building in Droitwich reminded me of the old warehouse in Cape Town, South Africa where I met Cedric and Cecil.

17.
My first job

Buitenkant Street, Cape Town was where the warehouse was.

Full of leather hides of all shapes and sizes, the company had been in buisness since 1890 and was in one of the oldest parts of Cape Town. The hides were tanned out at Western Tanning in Paarl where the cattle were taken to be slaughtered and the skins removed.

Most of the clients were the large number of small shoemakers in District Six and Observatory and Mowbray where they made all manner of shoes from moccasins to big boots and they all needed leather.

Clive was the salesman. Clive Carter would always give you a good deal. I watched him many times as a customer would handle a nice piece of leather and Clive always seemed to know if they were going to ask for a discount or a special price. He would mentally add back enough to the price to allow him to give the discount the lady asked for.

Clive's father was the Director of the company whilst Mr Kahn was the real work-horse and with Miss Mawman completed the team until I arrived, all fresh faced and aged only twenty-seven for my first real job as Accountant!.

Very excited I was and raring to go, until I found out that the systems were very old fashioned indeed. Hand-written ledgers with carbon paper if you wanted a copy, and no mechanisation at all.

It was 1969 and the most modern technology I had seen to date were the amazing comptometer machines which had been used at Mobil Oil, where I had been part of the audit team.

I spent the first day with Miss Mawman, letting her explain to me how the system worked, knowing all along that I had been employed specifically to bring it into the modern age.

Miss Mawman was a real character - rather like Agatha Christie's Miss Marple always dressed in a grey top and skirt and wore a hat when she went home. She was 60 when she retired and had been at Mercantile Holdings, as the company was called, for nearly forty years.

My interview had been with a tall distinguished gentleman called Denis Woolacott, who was not only Company Secretary but Group Company Secretary and originally hailed from Port Elizabeth, another major coastal City 200 odd miles away.

He had an office upstairs in the dusty top of the warehouse and he was lucky because he had a window and could see the outside world. He showed me to my office which had no such luxury and was small and dark with a desk, but it had one over-riding benefit: it was mine, all mine.

The only way up to these offices was a dark stairway at the back of the building, and I got quite fit striding though the racks of leather to the back down the stairs and along through the other cubby-hole offices on either side to where the Cashier, Miss Mawman sat, keeping a beady eye on everyone.

The warehouse was very old, but of course the warm climate meant that any holes in the roof or the walls only made for better ventilation and that helped in a country that ranged from warm in the winter through to very hot in the summer.

I worked very hard and enjoyed it, often working late upstairs in my office - almost always with Denis Woolacott also working on some legal document or something. There were often old customers coming in to see us and it was unusual for there not to be a new person for me to meet each day.

Invariably they would come upstairs and sit in my office asking how things were going and so I didn't notice really that one particular chap seemed to be there quite a lot. I struck up quite a friendship with him and we used to discuss the leather market and how prices were going up because inflation was always a significant factor in South Africa.

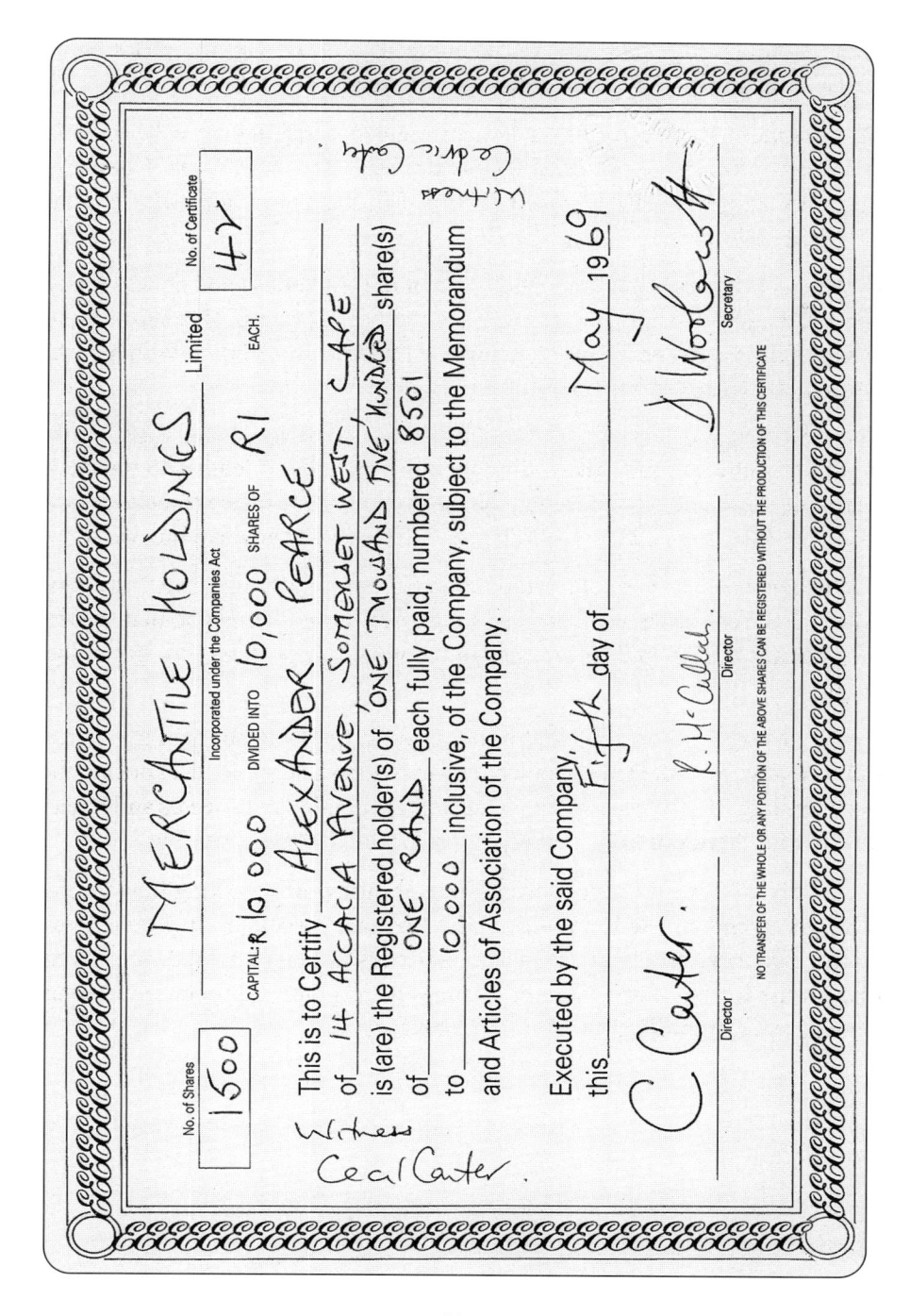

MERCANTILE HOLDINGS Limited

Incorporated under the Companies Act

No. of Shares: 1500

No. of Certificate: 47

CAPITAL: R 10,000 DIVIDED INTO 10,000 SHARES OF R1 EACH.

This is to Certify ALEXANDER PEARCE of 14 ACCACIA Avenue SOMERSET WEST, CAPE is (are) the Registered holder(s) of ONE THOUSAND FIVE HUNDRED share(s) of ONE RAND each fully paid, numbered 8501 to 10,000 inclusive, of the Company, subject to the Memorandum and Articles of Association of the Company.

Executed by the said Company, this Fifth day of May 1969

Witness
Cedric Carter

C Carter. — Director
R. McCulloch — Director
J Woolworth — Secretary

Witness
Cecil Carter.

NO TRANSFER OF THE WHOLE OR ANY PORTION OF THE ABOVE SHARES CAN BE REGISTERED WITHOUT THE PRODUCTION OF THIS CERTIFICATE

18.
Getting Advice

It was always at the end of the day - maybe ten minutes or so before I planned to go home - when my old friend would come in and sit down and ask how things were.

One particular evening Denis Woolacott came through to the office and greeted my friend as Mr Cedric.

Denis said "I see you've met Neil". "Oh yes" I said "we are already old friends!"

"Do you think he will do well ?" Denis asked Cedric.

"Oh yes he will, but you will have to hold on to him because others will want his services", Mr Cedric replied. A wise old boy I thought because I was as a young accountant already receiving offers from other companies to move to them. This was not exceptional at all because it happened to everyone.

"Denis, I don't think you ought to have moved into Port Elizabeth" said Cedric.

"Why not?" asked Denis. "Well, I think the motor trade will flourish there and leather will suffer. Cape Town is the place", he replied, and so it went on and I realised that we were getting some really good perceptive advice.

I thought Cedric was a good chap!

"How long have you been associated with Mercantile", I asked him. "Oh, quite a long time" he replied.

Denis had already gone back to his office and I went to check with him whether he would lock up and Denis casually said "what did you think of Cedric?"

"I was most impressed to be honest because he talks a lot of good solid sense, don't you think?" I replied. "Yes I do - but how long have you known him.?" he said.

"A couple of months - I suppose he comes in to see me most evenings", I replied. Denis said "I think you'd better come in here and sit down" as he led me to his office.

"As far I know, you and I are the only people he talks to but that is not surprising because he has been dead for nearly fifty years ! Cedric and his brother Cecil formed this company in 1906 and for many years it flourished until the two brothers had a row and fell out", continued Denis.

"Cecil was so upset that he killed himself. He hanged himself at the top of those stairs over there, and only weeks after his funeral Cedric joined him by committing suicide in exactly the same spot. They are both now ghosts and they both come back regularly to try and find the other.

"You are obviously receptive to ghosts as you didn't even realise that he was a ghost. I didn't, at first, until I realised that the building was locked and I can see the top of the stairs from here so there is no way he could get in or out.

"They are twins and I think were inseparable and they desperately want to come back to be as they were, but it is not possible".

"You mean to tell me that the man I have been talking to these evenings is a ghost", I exclaimed.

"Yes indeed and I think there are two of them and we can't tell them apart because they are identical twins", replied Denis.

"Haven't you noticed me say at Board meetings that I think I will sleep on that decision or I will check with our attorneys? Well, of course, I have checked with Cedric or Cecil and as you can see they are very sensible and give me great advice".

"I understand exactly now but how in the world of goodness can we help them?" I asked.

"I think they just want to be together again but how can we help?"

Some weeks passed and one evening I was again working late. I was in my office with Cedric and, being lazy, I phoned Denis just to see when he was going and he said that he was asking Cecil's advice about the move to Port Elizabeth and I realised - with the hairs on the back of my neck standing on end - that Cedric was in my office and Cecil was with Denis. What an opportunity!

"Denis we must sign those share certificates urgently" I said, "but we need two witnesses. Why don't we do that now and go through to the Boardroom office to do it".

Without thinking, without pausing, without disturbing anything I said to Cedric, "Please bring a pen as we need you to witness a signature", and Denis heard what I said and all four of us went into Sandy Pearce's Boardroom office and signed and then witnessed the share certificates.

I stood up and said "Thank you gentlemen and looked up as these two wonderful brothers went forward and hugged one another turning round and round and round.

"Can we be friends again", said one - I don't know which and "of course!" said the other and these two amazing men walked off to the head of the stairs and, just as they got there, they turned and said in unison to Denis and I, "Thank you gentlemen" and they swept off down the stairs and we never saw them again.

We had brought them together and they were as one again and we can prove that because their two signatures are on those Share certificates - very similar but subtly different signatures nevertheless.

Many people don't believe Denis and I when we tell the story but we don't care because we feel we did something really useful for those wonderful gentlemen.

They are often seen round town, walking up Adderley Street in the centre of Cape Town and if you said to another passer by.

"Those two gentlemen are ghosts, you know!!" they would have replied, "don't be so daft - I saw them, just as you did."

19.
Nether Kineddar

There were always doubts cast by historians and literary experts as to who actually wrote the Waverley Novels. No one doubts that Sir Walter Scott wrote the other great works but because the style was slightly different, people thought that, maybe, it was an impostor trying to pass himself off as the great master.

Sir Walter was unquestionably one of the greatest of Scotland's writers ever from Scotland writing a number of major historical works in the seventeenth century, and is only rivalled in fame outside Scotland by my namesake the infamous Robbie Burns.

I met Sir Walter at a house called Nether Kineddar in Saline, Fife in Scotland in 1977.

We had invited a charming couple called Sue and Roddy Jones to dinner at our house - Preston Place (sometimes referred to as Peyton Place because of the great parties held there). We talked about everything that evening and when we got onto ghosts, another guest poo-pooed the whole idea, saying it was nonsense and just stories made up to attract attention. With that Roddy said how he wished that was true, because then he wouldn't have to put up with the dreadful noise every night which came from the upper rooms at Nether Kineddar.

"Who is making the noise?", asked our guest and Roddy replied "We don't know. All we do know is that every evening there is a frightful thumping and banging and the furniture is being thrown about in the upstairs rooms".

"Nonsense" exclaimed our friend and Roddy said "you come next week and you can hear for yourself". Well, we were all invited exactly a week later.

We all had a few drinks to relax and I suggested that we close the front and back doors and then count the people in the house. Sue came through from the kitchen and that made a round eight of us including Colin and Kitty

McCrone who were both local practising doctors so we were in good company if anyone needed any medical attention. We all looked in various rooms to ensure there were no children or hoaxsters playing any pranks.

The dinner was so good that we really had forgotten about ghosts and our sceptical friends were looking a little smug when the banging started. It was as if three or four men were humping tables about upstairs, scraping chairs and generally being pretty rough about it. "There you are", said Roddy, "I have to put up with that every night!"

"Let's go upstairs", said I and we set off with the noise getting louder as we went.

The dining room - like the kitchen - was on the ground floor, so we had to climb a landing and then make our way up another very narrow straight staircase to the top.

As we entered the room, there was only one man there, but he was cross. He was pushing the table first to one side and then the other. He put a chair first here, then there, at which we heard him say "Where is the fireplace?"

I walked in and was ready to ask him many questions, but as I stepped into the room I became rooted to the spot and could neither move forward nor back - nor could I utter a word. It was a dreadful experience, for my chest felt tight and I was engulfed in cold; it was like being set in solid ice.

Thank goodness it only lasted a few seconds until the rest of our friends arrived and everything popped, like a blocked ear which clears, and all the furniture was still and the man was nowhere to be seen.

We counted and there were eight of us including Sue, who was at the bottom of the stairs.

"We must find his fireplace", I said and I started tapping the walls until there was a hollow sound from behind. "We must open this up, Roddy, because he is angry and won't rest until his fireplace is open again.", I said.

"Didn't I read somewhere that Sir Walter Scott is supposed to have written the Waverley novels here, and then after a row about them with his publisher he burnt them - presumably in this fireplace" said our sceptical guest

Nether Kinneddar

warming to the situation.

Nether Kinneddar had been the home of Lord Kinneddar, who was Sir Walter Scott's literary agent and publisher and this would have been an ideal spot to write, with the wonderful views back towards Edinburgh over the Forth.

"If he can't see the fireplace he has no chance whatever of finding the ashes to prove what happened. That's why he is so unhappy and that's why he's making such a fuss to attract your attention", I said.

"Well, we will see" said Roddy and we all went downstairs.

"I don't want to be discourteous, Roddy, but these stairs don't seem to be in keeping with rest of the house", I said to our host and he admitted that the previous owner had taken out a circular staircase up to the top, because his wife didn't like it.

"Well there is a lot of your trouble, because Sir Walter can't come and go as he would wish and he is grumpy simply because of that", said I.

The following week Roddy called me at work and said "Come round tonight - I've got a new whisky for you to taste", and although I am great lover of whisky, I suspected it was something else that he wanted to show me.

20.
Whisky

He handed me the whisky as I arrived and we strode up to the top floor straight away.

There, in the wall where I had tapped, a true craftsman stood admiring his work which had uncovered a beautiful old fireplace with a tiny grate and very slim chimney as you often find in these old houses.

A beam formed the mantelpiece and as picturesque a setting I have rarely seen.

We moved the table further across so that it faced the window out across the garden, away towards Edinburgh and placed the armed back chair in just the right spot.

I stood in the very same spot where I had been rooted before and there was no iciness, no tight chest, just a warm and relaxed sensation.

"You have done well, Roddy", said I

"Thanks to our friend, here" said Roddy

"There is the fireplace - didn't I tell you so!", said the craftsman.

And I said to Roddy "Our friend here doesn't have a whisky" and I handed him my glass, which was still half full of the new whisky Roddy had invited me to taste.

"Let's go and fetch the bottle" said Roddy and we both turned adding "we will be back to finish it with you very soon."

"You are very kind" was all he said.

I waited at the foot of the stairs, talking to Sue who was saying "we have had no noise at all from upstairs, you know, since we opened up that fireplace".

"That's wonderful. - We must go and share the rest of the bottle with our friend". I said "By the way who did the restoration for you, Sue?"

"Roddy did it all", she said

And as I opened my mouth to say the obvious, Roddy arrived and we went together upstairs where, on the table, was an empty whisky glass and Roddy said, "I think he enjoyed the whisky."

21.
Man at the road side

In all the cars I have been lucky enough to drive I have kept a visitors' book to record all the people who have travelled in the car, and there are many interesting names there. But one name stands out as particularly special.

One evening as I came home in the car towards Saline, I saw at the roadside an old man who seemed completely exhausted and was struggling to make any forward progress at all.

It was a foul night - with fresh snow falling and I was very keen to get home into the warmth - but I simply couldn't pass this man by. I stopped the car and said "would you like a lift? I'm going your way!", and without a word he clambered into the car.

I had to reach over him to draw the door to, and settle him in. He was frozen, literally frozen, his clothes were stiff, his trousers hard and his beard was encrusted with ice.

This poor man was in a bad way and would surely have died very soon had he not found someone to help him.

"Where do you live?", I asked as I switched the car heater up to maximum and he struggled to reply "anywhere you are going is fine with me, sir."

I could almost feel the cold being beaten back by the warmth from the car heater and he started to relax - apologising that his beard was a bit wet.

"Where do you live?" I asked again and got no reply.

As we neared my home I said he must come in and he declined; a jellie - piece was all he needed. Now a jellie - piece, in Scotland, is sandwich made with jam or jelly, so I left him in the car as I went in to ask my wife to get him a jellie-piece. I knew he would be all right in the car, especially as it was now firmly in our garage, and when I returned with the food he was very grateful.

"You must sign our visitors book", I said.   "No I will not" he insisted.

"Why ever not?" said I "everybody does". "No I will not", he repeated whilst polishing off the rest of the jellie-piece.

"Come on, sign the book for me" I pleaded with him, and his answer was, "Sir, I can neither read nor write, so if you would do me the service and write my name for me, I would be most grateful".

And so I wrote in our visitors book, slowly, the name William John Reid as he watched on in awe.

"Is that my name?", he asked.

"Yes indeed it is - and a fine name it is", I said

"Its looks well in the writing", he said and he was so proud of his name. "It is the first time I have ever seen it - I can now die a happy man".

I tried to persuade him to come in and join us but he would not do so.

"I live just a short way away" he said "and the wind is in my back and I have seen my name. I am a happy man thanks to you, sir", and he walked off with his shoulders held high.

I often wondered who that man was. Is it possible that he knew I had a visitors' book and would help him with his name? No. That was far too far fetched.

22.
The Story is not yet over

Lily and I keep in touch in unusual ways. Near her grave is a little garden and I have often taken plants there, particularly perennials, so that as the years go by they will be a recurring reminder to us both.

I took a cutting from the little garden at her grave, which I brought back with me to my office in Mamble in Worcestershire. I started it growing on the windowsill of my office and over a period of weeks it eventually took root and grew strong. I transplanted it down to a special spot overlooking the fishpond I had dug two years ago.

I had to put it out of reach of my ducks which I have reared since they were ducklings. Although they greet me with great warmth when I do go down there every day to feed them - they are no respecters of property and eat everything in sight so I had to find a spot out of reach - and that takes some doing.

There is an archway, set back into the hill, which houses a natural spring and the ground round it is vertical, so into that I have set inset a little ledge and Lily grows in safety, and, I may say, some style.

Every time now I go to see Lily's grave I take a small cutting and bring one back so that the two spots are interconnected. One day when I was at her grave, I noticed that someone else was also tendering it and I left my card saying "To the person tending Lily's grave; please contact me."

I am delighted to say that Mrs Alex Southeran called me some ten days later and I have since met her and her amazing husband, David, who lives a wonderful life mainly roaming the dales, often at night, totally at home with all the animals there.

He is a highly educated man, with a wonderful library of books and records and items of interest, and when I visit him we compare notes on everything, but of course, especially Lily.

The story of Lily is not yet over because there are still many unanswered questions.

23.
Mary Queen of Scots

I admit to being in love with Mary Queen of Scots.

She was a wonderful lady who had a very tragic life.

She was born in Stirling Castle in central Scotland in 1542

and when she was only six days old her father, the King of Scotland, died.

And so, not yet a week old, she became Mary, Queen of Scots.

From that day on, it seemed that men and women fought over her welfare and safety and almost always for their own ends.

At the age of five or six she was sent to France for safety and lived in the Champagne country, looked after by her mother, Mary of Guise.

When she was barely old enough, she married Francis, the Dauphin of France in an arranged wedding designed only to cement friendly relations between Scotland and France.

Francis was a sickly child and apparently suffered from all known ailments. Some say he was mad but he was destined to become the King of France when his father, Henry II, was tragically killed in a jousting contest, with his successful opponent becoming the most unpopular man in France for accidentally killing his own King.

So at only sixteen years old, Mary became Queen of France as well as Queen of Scotland.

Her husband the king was a chronic invalid and by all accounts he went mad and died after only two years on the throne, so Mary became a widow at eighteen.

At this time there was turmoil in Scotland, with infighting between the clansmen all vying to oust Mary from the throne and get rid of the Consort who ruled on her behalf.

Mary returned by sea and landed at Leith, the port for Edinburgh wearing all her French finery having just come from the finest court in France. She was

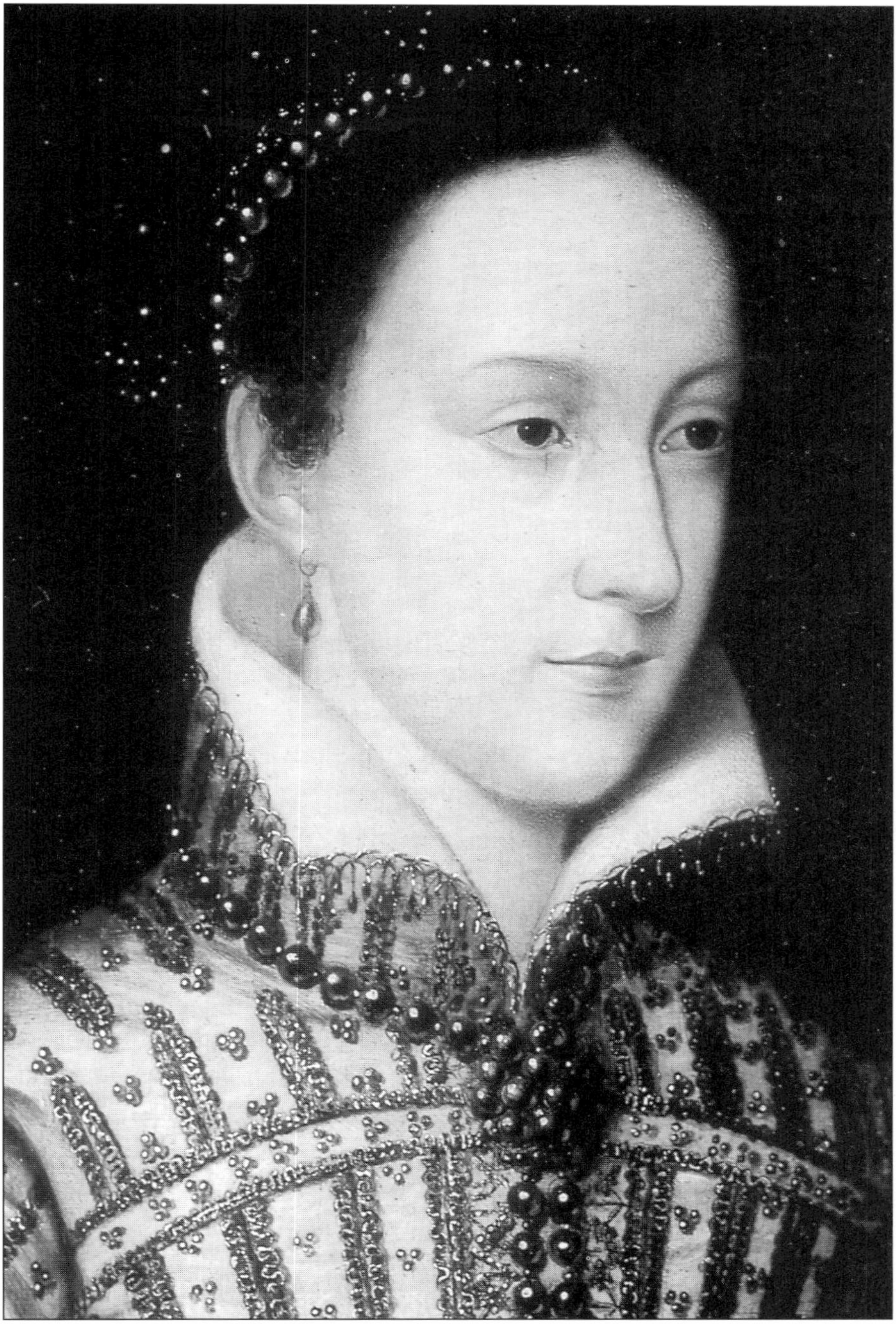

met by an oxcart to carry her though the dank, wet streets of Edinburgh to the Castle at the top end of the Royal Mile.

She must have been so miserable and of course none of her subjects recognised their Queen who had, remember, been their Queen for nearly twenty years already.

Mary and her few friends slowly imposed themselves on the unruly Scots lords and, over two or three years, a reasonable court was established.

She had a great struggles and survived many battles fought over her. She was captured and imprisoned on a number of occasions one of her best remembered sojourns being on an island in Loch Leven, which is the subject of many tales.

She apparently escaped after her food servant smuggled her a key under her napkin.

Of course, Mary had an undeniable right to the throne of England. Henry the Eighth had six wives and many argue, especially Catholics like Mary, that divorce was not legal and therefore all his children by every Queen, after the first one, were illegitimate.

This made Elizabeth, the crowned Queen of England, illegitimate in their eyes and Mary her cousin was therefore next in line through her grandfather Henry VIIth and therefore, the rightful Queen of England.

Queen Elizabeth was acutely aware of this and therefore hated her cousin Mary. She went to extraordinary lengths to keep her out of England in case she rallied Catholic support for her cause which could easily have swept her to power.

So much so that she eventually tricked Mary into travelling to England secretly to meet her, and Elizabeth's men captured and imprisoned her for nineteen long years before eventually having her beheaded.

What a wonderful way to treat your cousin and what a dreadful time it must have been to live.

I have met Mary Queen of Scots on five occasions, and it is all because I have a service to perform for her.

Either that or I failed to serve her, not, I am sure, out of fear or cowardice but because I was simply not at the right place at the right time.

24.
Linlithgow Palace

I was returning to my brother's house near the tiny village of Kilconquhar, in Fife, one afternoon when I had a sudden urge to make a detour to Linlithgow Palace, which I had never seen but which was reputed to be haunted by Mary Queen of Scots.

I had the afternoon free so I headed off towards Linlithgow, which is not far from Edinburgh but nevertheless a little off the beaten track.

I found the town quite easily but struggled to find the Palace as I went past it two or three times before someone showed me the very narrow road which led to it.

I arrived at maybe four o'clock in the afternoon and was surprised that there was only one other car in the parking area.

I went in and found a rather fat lady in the little shop saying, "You can buy a ticket for three pounds but it's not haunted you know", which I felt was a fine example of salesmanship.

Well, I was as disappointed as she expected me to be, with only a ruin of a building with no furnishings at all and whilst I dutifully went up to the top of each tower, I saw and felt nothing.

I did, however, meet a party of three Americans who were rather noisily taking pictures of each other rather than Linlithgow Palace.

I made some remark about their making so much noise it was no wonder the ghost did not appear, and I told them that I had come to see the ghost of Mary Queen of Scots, who is supposed to haunt the Palace.

"I know that she used to stay here and, in particular, used to worship in a little chapel within the Palace", I told them. They were intrigued but unconvinced.

After a lot of struggle, seemingly going round and round without finding it, I eventually went through an inner door and there was the chapel.

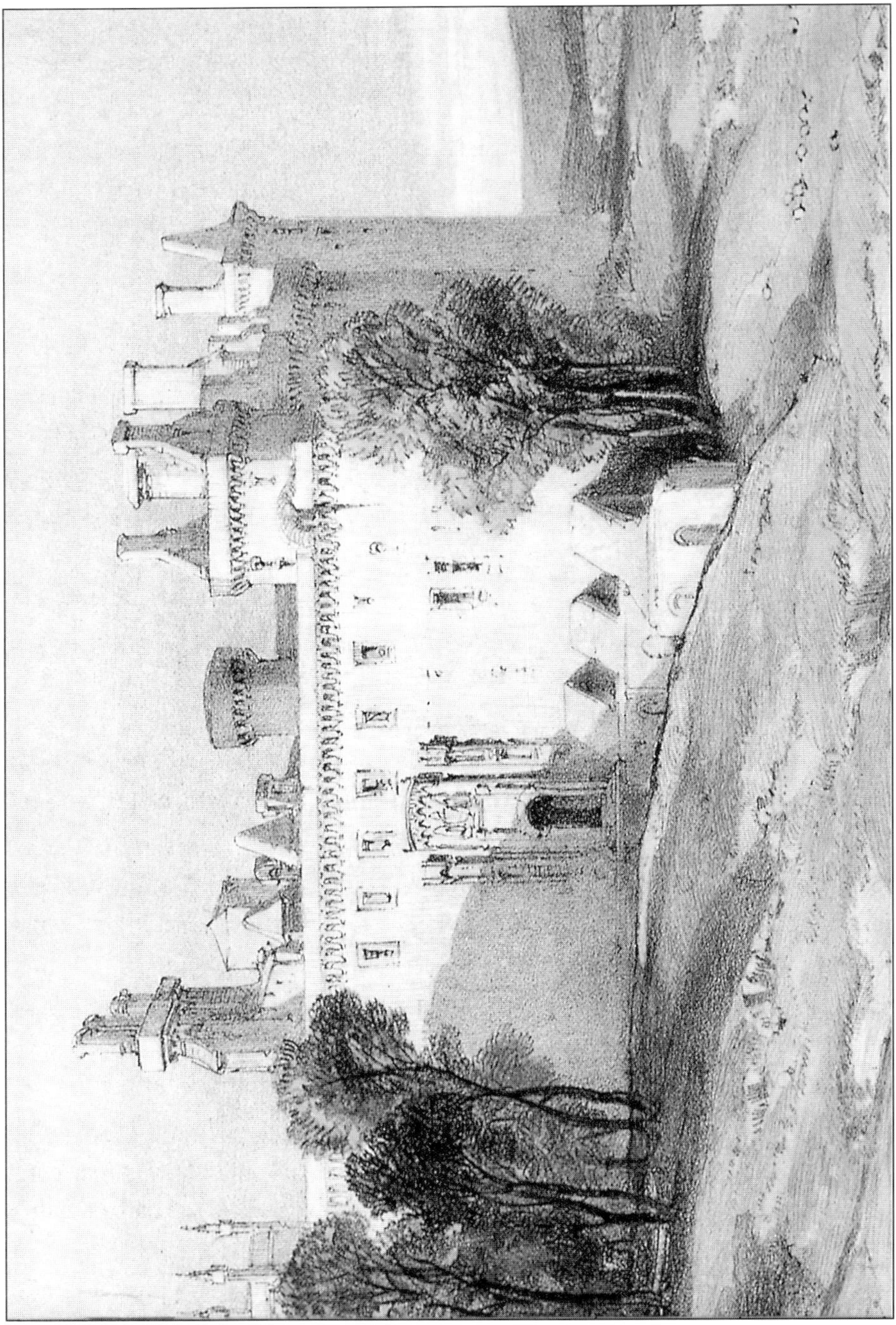

Just four walls now and a very high roof but there was a strange gallery set in to one wall, which was higher that one storey but not as high as two, if you understand me.

There was a railing so that you could stand there and look down into the chapel and I had an urge to go up there.

It must be connected I thought and, being very careful to retrace my steps, I went in search of the missing link to get there.

Now these Palaces had many circular staircases and unless you have a built in compass, you very soon lose the sense of direction; "where is North?". I simply couldn't tell and to make matters worse, the exits from these circular staircases do not all come out at the same angle or in fact on the same floor.

I tried and tried to find the way to that gallery and eventually, because I was getting tired, I went to the shop at the bottom and said "Please could you help me find the way to the gallery overlooking the chapel".

"That is very easy", she replied, "follow me!" and I started off after her but as I did so, as often happens, I started to limp because when I am tired the one leg is a lot better than the other.

This slowed the fat lady down and, although we walked a long way, we couldn't find it and she was amazed. "You stay here and I will find it and come back for you, although why you are going to all this fuss is beyond me".

Well she came back in maybe five minutes saying, "I can't find it. You will just have to leave." I said, "that is ridiculous - you will have give me my money back!"

That made her take notice and she said "I will call my husband" and off she went. Her husband was just as confident of finding it - which should have simplicity itself, especially as he knew every nook and cranny of the Palace.

Well he returned after a few minutes, he said "I give up", and just as I was getting cross and about to demand my money back the three Americans arrived saying "we have seen a gallery above the chapel but we had a terrible job finding our way out."

"Show me the way", I said and they took me straight to the gallery, to find the fat lady and her husband standing below us in the chapel, looking very pleased with themselves. "We knew you would find it eventually" said the fat lady.

"Remember you must leave by six o clock!"

I was thanking the Americans and pointing out to them that you could see though the tall windows, which had no longer any glass in them, towards the main gate and we were all admiring the symmetry of the architecture when the tall figure of a lady appeared inside the gate.

I first spotted her and then touched the arm of the American lady who whispered, "Be quiet, Luke, there is someone coming!"

We saw though the same window the main gates being closed, as our lady walked straight for us towards the natural door, but unfortunately she went out of our sight, blocked by the wall of the chapel.

I began to feel very funny and looked at Luke, who was as pale as a sheet. "You can't leave now, Luke", said I, as over his shoulder I saw the most beautiful and radiant lady approach through the archway on to our gallery.

She came and stood between Luke and me and looked demurely down into the Chapel. She was tall and graceful, beautifully dressed in a bodice waistcoat and long dark skirt, all of which were richly embroidered. Her face was serene and beautiful and I recognised her immediately from the many paintings of her.

She said "I am very grateful to you for finding this precious place for me. I have looked for many years but no one has ever matched my determination to find it"

She stood in silence, oblivious to our presence as her eyes searched the floor of the chapel, inch by inch.

"I am satisfied now", she said. "thank you again kind sir!" and she swept past us towards that archway and was gone.

Luke was now white and his wife much the same as I said "You realise that was Mary Queen of Scots and I think we have done her a great service. Poor soul, she has been looking for this spot for over three hundred years and I was frustrated after less than an hour!"

The little boy with them said "who was that nice lady? - There she goes again!" and we all saw Mary striding happily towards the main gate.

"Oh there you are!", shouted the fat lady's husband - "we have been looking everywhere for you. The main gate was shut at six and we want to go home."

"You mean that no one has been after six o clock", I asked

"That's right and it is now six thirty", said she with feeling.

"How did that lady get out then?" said the little boy and his parents grabbed him and headed to the archway and downstairs.

I was still tired and my hip hurt but I followed the sounds of the Americans and in a relatively short time was at the shop.

"Thank goodness", said the man "we thought we had lost you forever".

"You didn't sell a ticket to a beautiful young lady, did you?" I checked.

"We did not!", replied the fat lady "we are not allowed to sell after six o clock and anyway the doors were locked!"

"Mary Queen of Scots has been here so many times she doesn't need a ticket now", I said. "Keep an eye out for her in that gallery - she knows how to get there now."

The next day in the papers an article described how three Americans had seen Mary Queen of Scots at Linlithgow Palace, although for some strange reason they didn't mention me!

25.
Reims

Many years earlier in 1988, I went with a coach party of office colleagues to France, (and to be more specific) to the Champagne country near Reims to the North East of Paris.

It was a very happy party and it was my good luck to sit next to a stunning young girl called Helen, who had joined the party at the very last moment because of a cancellation.

We set off from Kidderminster at two in the afternoon, and as we were a party of wine lovers setting off on holiday to see and taste many interesting French wines, it was not at all surprising that the first cork was heard to pop just as the wheels of the coach started to roll.

We were in high spirits throughout the journey and eventually arrived for an evening meal at a hotel in the outskirts of Reims, where we straggled in to be booked in at the reception.

As Helen was rather tired, I picked her up and carried her in, rather like a husband traditionally carries his wife over the threshold, and this caused great amusement to about fifty German tourists who were, I think, on a similar trip to ours.

When, later, our party of thirty went down to our enormous table, the Germans started singing their wedding song and, much as Helen and I protested that we were not getting married, in fact we weren't even yet good friends, nothing would shake the Germans from their belief.

As the evening progressed, Helen and I took the line of least resistance, saying, "If you can't beat them join them," and we thoroughly enjoyed playing the part.

The evening ended to a great cheer as I carried Helen up the stairs and deposited her at the door of her room, where she collapsed if in a mixture of fatigue and intoxication in a deep sleep.

As I got some help from the rest of the party, a great cheer went up from the Germans as we carried Helen into her room onto her bed and she was fast asleep by the time we shut the door.

After breakfast, I went for a short walk to buy the usual postcards and was intrigued to see one referring to Mary of Guise, who apparently had lived here. She was, as you all know, the mother of Mary Queen of Scots and I asked someone if they knew about Mary.

All I could discover was that she was known as Marie Stuart here and someone said that there was a champagne named after her.

Later in the day we had three or four visits to the vineyards, and the cellars of the various champagne houses. They were all excellent in their way, with the best, as you might expect, at the magnificent head office of Moet et Chandon, the biggest of them all.

As we were leaving, Helen called me to one side and said she had lost her purse. It must have been left it at one of the previous cellars. All the others, of course, wanted to continue with the trip, so I volunteered to take Helen back to find her purse, saying to her as we went, that I had something else to find.

The concierge found us a taxi and we explained to the driver in my best French where we needed to go. The driver like everyone in France, assumed we were eloping or certainly heading for a frisky afternoon somewhere, but we persuaded him to take us back the way we had come, and fortunately we recovered the purse on the second stop.

We had agreed to meet the rest of the party at Reims Cathedral later that afternoon but we now had time to explore, and I took Helen in search of Marie Stuart.

We asked the driver whether he knew anything about Mary Queen of Scots and although I am sure I described Mary's marriage to Phillippe the Dauphin of France, it was only when I said Marie Stuart that he exclaimed "Rue Marie Stuart!!" He knew a street called Marie Stuart.

We set off to find it and this seemed to trigger his memory as he told us of "le tragedie" of the "jeune petite Reine de France" - the young, small queen of France.

We arrived at Rue Marie Stuart and as I could see the Cathedral towering above the city, within easy walking distance, I paid off the taxi driver and Helen and I walked up a street a little off the beaten track.

We saw a plaque on the wall saying *Champagne de Marie Stuart* and we realised we had stumbled on the headquarters of the company selling this champagne.

I rang the bell and asked very nicely if we could enquire about the *Champagne de Marie Stuart*, and got a reception which was, to say the least, frosty. I think we would have stayed on the doorstep trying to inveigle our way in for ever, had I not said "But the champagne is for Mademoiselle ici" - for Helen standing beside me.

The Director of the company was summonsed, and as soon as he arrived, immediately showed extraordinary deference to my young companion, seeming almost to recognise Helen. We were ushered in and given the Royal treatment, with first call always to Helen.

I then saw a magnificent life size portrait of Mary Queen of Scots, called, of course, Marie Stuart and as I turned towards Helen, it was obvious that they had all noticed the uncanny likeness of Helen to that portrait.

Did they think this was Mary returned to visit them ?

Did they maybe think that Helen was a descendant of Mary's? They clearly held her in considerable awe.

Helen was oblivious to all the attention, saying only, to me, "They seem awfully nice people here!"

I asked about Mary and whether she had lived here and they, of course, replied that she was part of the House of Guise. She eventually married the Dauphin of France when she was sixteen until his tragic death two years later when she was eighteen.

Helen was also eighteen years old.

We tasted the specially poured champagne and were given a complimentary bottle of it and we warmly thanked the Director, who gave his very special card to Helen, "You must come and visit us anytime, Mademoiselle."

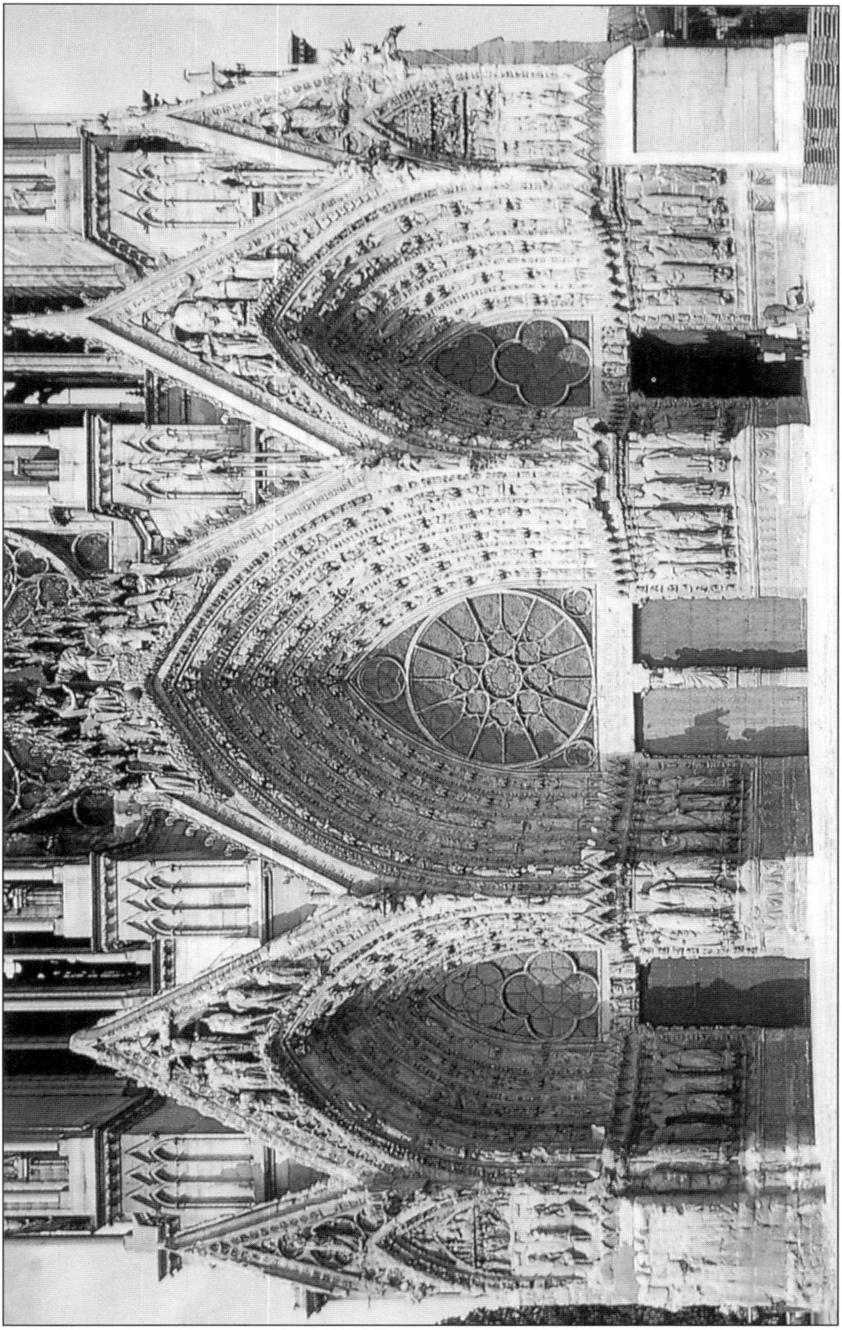

We then set off towards the Cathedral and walked what turned out to be quite a long way through the streets, till all of a sudden we were outside it and I asked a lady selling leaflets "Can we go in?"

"Of course but please speak to Madame Pompadour inside the main door", she replied.

As she was saying this she excitedly tugged her own companion's arm and pointed towards Helen, who again just walked casually beside me. The companion set off at a run for the cathedral and hurtled inside in undue haste.

I started to feel an intense excitement as we walked towards the massive doors of the Cathedral, which were (of course) closed, as are the main doors of most cathedrals.

To my amazement, they started to open as Helen and I walked towards them.

I think I was invisible. All eyes were on Helen and as we walked in I could hardly breathe for excitement, as the people all around us looked on in awe of Helen. This surely must be Marie Stuart returned to visit them.

Helen and I walked round as tourists might, and I asked questions of them about Marie Stuart, and they all looked in puzzlement as if to say "surely you already know her well?"

We went to the front of the massive altar and I stood, exhilarated, with enormous happiness and a swelling in my chest as if something wonderful was happening - it was almost mystical - even magical and although Helen was interested and enjoying it, I could sense that she felt no special excitement at all.

We walked back towards the main door, and thanked Madame for telling us about the Cathedral and she wished Mademoiselle well, with instructions to me "look after her well when you take her back to Scotland."

I had not previously mentioned Scotland, and I have no discernible accent, so this surprised me, but Helen said "she always was a bit of a nag, Madame, always telling me to look after myself".

As we swept out into the square we saw the rest of the party approaching and rushed over to them and were quickly engulfed by them.

I wanted to go back and was disappointed to see the doors were now shut. There was a queue, albeit a short one, at the little entrance at the side of the main doors.

As I went in, it felt cold, and Madame who had spent nearly half an hour with Helen and me didn't seem to recognise me. I asked her if she would open the doors, because it would be marvellous.

"Oh no Monsieur", she said, "the doors never open - the last time they were opened was when Marie Stuart left for Scotland".

"Let me see the doors", I said, and I went to the base of the doors and the massive hinges were encrusted with rust and had not been moved in many decades.

Madame looked me straight in the eye and said, "You see, Monsieur, you must be mistaken. The doors of Reims Cathedral have been closed since 1561."

As I returned to the party, there was Helen telling the others how wonderful it was in the cathedral, and how you could see everything - it was so light and airy inside.

26.
Flight of Fancy

1561 was the year Mary Queen of Scots returned to Scotland and I was determined to meet her.

Imagination is a powerful force and I have become able to transport myself purely by imagination to the most faraway places and times - if you believe it - you are there.

I lived during the seventies in a wonderful little village called Saline in Fife where, you will recall I met Sir Walter Scott, and Saline in turn was close to Stirling which used to be the main stronghold of Scotland, and some say, the real capital.

I had also lived in Edinburgh and knew it well, so when I woke up in 1567 I found myself in familiar surroundings near Linkfield House, just across the road from the Musselburgh golf links, one of the first places where the game was ever played.

I was wearing shorts and had lots of hair, so I guessed I was maybe eighteen or so, and as I walked back towards Edinburgh a group of horsemen were riding the same way at a leisurely pace.

"Young man!", shouted one of them, "We need good strong young chaps like you follow us", and I saw no reason not to follow this bold looking man, who I later learned was James Hepburn, Earl of Bothwell, the man destined to marry Mary Queen of Scots. I immediately took to him as he had an air of leadership and a charisma that set him above others.

There was a cart amongst the party, drawn by an old horse and I leapt aboard leaving behind me Musselburgh, which I grew to know very well later when I was at school there.

I was getting used to seeing places many years removed from when I knew them but I also understood that my knowledge of later years' events could help the people currently here, not that I would give them any unfair advantage, merely give them the benefit of my knowledge.

"Where are you going?" I asked. "To see our Queen, of course" they cried, and I was overjoyed! "Where will she be?", I asked, "She has called us all to Dunfermline Abbey in Fife, where she has gathered a meeting, but we are not sure how to get there. Which way should we go?". Without thinking I said "We must cross at Queensferry".

I knew that the Firth of Forth almost cut Scotland in half and although Dunfermline was just across the water, the only way to get there other than by ferry, was the very long trek via Kincardine Bridge which could take two to three days.

We wound through the country lanes until we came to the ferry at Queensferry, where I had crossed many times to go to school, thus knew it well. It is the point where Fife and the Lothians come closest and a natural spot for a ferry. This saved us at least two days of travel - all the way past Linlithgow and back over the bridge at Kincardine - but I wasn't aware of that at the time.

It took all day to cross, because the ferry was only big enough for 50 men and we were two hundred strong. So we rested and slept until the following morning when we set off for Dunfermline, which was where my father was born some 320 years later.

I didn't feel strange at all because at every point I knew something which was of value to the party. I remembered for instance the Hawes Inn at South Queensferry, where I had a wonderful dinner once with Archie Stewart and Minta and we made many important decisions about John Menzies at that hotel.

It is hidden away for good reason and I managed to smuggle the Earl of Bothwell there when he expressed the need for food and a little wine. Bothwell told me that he was certain we could not have reached Dunfermline in time, had it not been for the ferry which I knew about and he said "Mary will be pleased."

When we arrived at Dunfermline Abbey, Bothwell took me to him to meet Mary Queen of Scots, and I was overwhelmed because Mary remembered me and greeted me with warmth. I, of course, had met her at Linlithgow and helped her then, but for her to remember, was wonderful.

"Young sir - You look well!", said Mary, "and I, your Majesty am delighted to see you again" I replied. "Please may I be of service to you?" "Of course you may; what would you wish to do?", she inquired.

"Please do not travel south to England without Bothwell to guard you, because Elizabeth means to capture and imprison you." I said

"Stay here, I implore you, and I will ask the Lords to rally behind you till you are strong. By that time I, too, will be strong enough to go with you and Bothwell with an army to guard you. We will gather support in England from all good Catholics and you will eventually be Queen of England, as is your right!"

"I know I have to give you this message and I fear you will not heed it, but please listen to someone who knows what will happen." "Tell me more at Stirling " she said and I joined her in her apartments in Stirling Castle a week later.

Stirling Castle commands the whole centre of Scotland dominating the central plain which stretches almost from coast to coast, and it must have been a daunting sight for any opposing army.

The highest point around for many miles, the Castle was built on a huge outcrop of rock and the building came to the very extremity on three sheer sides. The fourth side looks out onto the joining of two rivers, another marvellous natural defence.

The walls were a continuation of the rock, so any person planning to scale them would be exhausted before they got very far.

Inside the castle there is a Palace and a huge chapel, and right at the very top the royal apartments. As if in complete contrast to the rest of the castle, in one corner there is a fabulous garden sheltered from the winds by the walls, and this was the haven where Mary chose to live. Safe, you would have thought from all danger, and having all the beauty of nature to enjoy in her favourite garden.

Although we were centuries apart, we were immediately attracted to one another, and we spent many happy hours together.

I like to think that I gave her a rare pleasure as Bothwell was a great warrior and friend, but never a great husband or lover.

Mary took my advice and, contrary to what the history books will tell you, was not captured by Elizabeth but lived on to see her son crowned as James VI of Scotland and James I of England.

History has always attributed Bothwell as the father of James I but maybe, just maybe, his father was an accountant on a mission of service to his beloved Queen.

Historians also have it that Bothwell and his retinue did not make it in time to Dunfermline. In their absence the other Lords persuaded Mary to go to England to make peace with Elizabeth, and we all know that she was captured, imprisoned for 19 years and then beheaded.

I know I have done my real service to my Queen!

27
The Three Cornered Hat

On many occasions we have spent a happy hour or two in the Talbot Inn, Bewdley which is owned by Paul who is quite a character. He always seems to know everybody in his pub by name, and many times I have tried to introduce him to someone new, and my goodness, it always turns out that they were in his pub yesterday and he already knows them well.

However, standing close to the fireplace at the back of the pub, there is a strange feeling of a line fault there which seems to split the room in two going across the bar area and right into the next door property called the Bailiff's House.

At Paul's invitation one night, I had a look round the pub which dates back to 1610 and has been in its present state for many years, so many of the fixtures and ornaments are very old.

Lots of people say it is haunted - but by whom and why?.

All pubs have cellars but this one has a very strange staircase right in the middle of the floor area that seems to disappear down into nowhere. I asked Paul if we could go down and he said "of course, but we have only just opened it up - it used to be closed completely."

It was eerie - seeming to go down into some place which you were not supposed to enter - and you always tread with great care and a fair bit of apprehension.

Someone, at one time, had used this regularly but now it had fallen into disuse.

"You ought to speak to Richard and Michelle next door at the Bailiff's House, because they keep getting an extra guest for dinner at one of their tables", said Paul.

"I will go and see them because the fault crosses straight into their property", I said.

83

I knocked on the door of the Bailiff's House and Richard and Michelle were very courteous and arranged immediately to have a little get together dinner there later that month.

They seemed, however, to be very concerned about their living quarters which were at the top of the house above the restaurant section, and I was invited to go up there and meet their young daughter Nicole who seemed to be ill at ease in her room.

I noticed certain pictures on the wall which caused me great distress - one in particular was like a mirror which gave off an evil sort of vibe.

I suggested they remove the mirror from the room and immediately young Nicole seemed happier. I don't know what it was but it needed to removed.

I invited my son Andrew and two girl friends who had expressed interest in ghosts to join us for dinner to see if any uninvited guest would join us.

First, however, I felt I should bring something old to the party to make whoever it was welcome so I went to the Old Emporium shop at the foot of Welch Gate to hunt for an old book for the purpose.

I was met by the proprietor who was very interested in my story and I said "let's go to a section of the shop which is not used too much", and he led me down into a lower room with the walls completely covered in old books.

Straight way I went to one which caught my eye, which turned out to be The Pilgrim's Progress - a book I had never read before. A very old and very dusty copy which my host told me would cost me one pound!

I was very happy with this transaction and when paying him, I noticed a three cornered hat in the window, and it seemed just the right thing to welcome our friend later that night.

I then went across the road into Load Street where Sheila May used to have an exclusive lingerie shop, but which had recently been taken over by an antique dealer.

I remember the shop very well as I was Sheila's Accountant and had to go there many times. It was an amazing shape being on the turn of the road. It was almost triangular with a tiny circular staircase at the very narrow end at the back.

I was one of the very few allowed up those stairs, past the changing rooms for the ladies, to the command headquarters at the top. These were lovely rooms with timber beams and uneven floors with lots of character. There I had many a cup of coffee and discussion with Sheila over business.

But today I just asked the owner "could I please look upstairs?" and as I got to the first floor, there, open on the desk right in front of me, was a beautiful old book and on the open page was a fine drawing of a three cornered hat! And - would you believe it - the book was none other that The Pilgrim's Progress.

This time I had to pay ten pounds for it, but as it was a beauty in good condition, I did not complain too much.

What a coincidence, I thought, particularly as I had no part at all in selecting the second book nor of opening it the three cornered hat.

I started to be excited about our dinner and what to expect as everything was apparently coming together.

I collected the two ladies, and we arrived for a pre-dinner drink. We sat downstairs directly in line with where I had earlier felt the fault line in the Talbot next door. It was strong and direct although not hostile in any way.

We moved upstairs almost exactly above where we had been below, and sat next to a large wooden post which obstructed just a little.

I felt strong feelings near this post and wasn't at all surprised when Michelle, our hostess, said "lots of people unfortunately don't like sitting there - it seems always to be too close to that post."

However, we all sat down and I was a little surprised that there were five places set and said so to Michelle who replied with a chuckle "Aren't you expecting some company?"

As we sat ourselves down I put the two copies of The Pilgrim's Progress and the three cornered black hat on the table where the fifth seat was.

We talked about all sorts of things during a beautifully presented dinner and noticed that a party of a dozen ladies had arrived, celebrating what was obviously a hen party, next door.

"Why have you put a three cornered hat there?" asked one of the ladies and we started to chat to them.

"Where are you from?" I asked.

"We're all from the Bewdley Information Centre, of course, but Elizabeth is down from Yorkshire and she is getting married very soon!". said the most forward one.

"Congratulations! and who is the lucky man?" I asked

"He is a Captain", she said with pride.

My ears pricked as I heard the word Captain - surely this couldn't be the girl who took Lily's place?.

I asked casually, "Is he a Balloonist that I have read about?".

"Oh yes indeed he is - and I have jumped for him many times since the tragic accident to Lily Cove".

"Yes I was very distressed to hear about that, Elizabeth. You must be careful when you jump to avoid any places where there is water."

"Thank you for warning me, kind sir," she said and I noticed that she went a little pale at my words.

We seemed very soon, however, to get into one very big party and intermingled so much so that I lost track of the books and the three cornered hat, with our other two guests asking Elizabeth all about Yorkshire and why she had come down to Bewdley.

Elizabeth seemed so happy and friendly and enjoyed every minute of the meal. At one stage Paul from next door arrived and Andrew scored a point by saying " Paul you haven't met Elizabeth have you?" and he replied " I haven't yet had that pleasure, but I sure she will come across for some real ale sometime soon."

When it came time to go there was the usual scurry over who was going to pay for what, and I said "let me have the bill for our party please". I was surprised, when it came, that it was only for four people.

The other ladies were just leaving, and I called the leader of their party who was settling their bill and asked "have you paid for Elizabeth who was sitting with us?."

"Who do mean", she said "there was no Elizabeth in our party." "But there was - she came from Haworth", I replied

"Oh no. You must be mistaken - we are all from Bewdley and we have paid all our bill!"

She was beginning to get a little hostile, as if I was trying to get her to pay for someone else, so I just left it at that.

"I must pay for Elizabeth", I said to Michelle "because she sat at our table by the three cornered hat."

"Yes she talked to us for ages" said Melissa and Nicola.

"I see no hat. Do you Andrew?" and sure enough there was no hat, no books and no Elizabeth.

Had we imagined it all or had there really been an extra guest .

I must remember to ask Paul the next time I see him. He never forgets a name or a face.

28.
Meeting Lily

My meeting with Elizabeth at the Talbot made me all the more determined to meet Lily again, and put the final pieces in the jigsaw together.

On many of the occasions I have visited Machin's, I would see Nancye Hobson, who is a great character of nearly eighty years of age, who invariably seems to be there.

She lives in a little attic house across the road from the shop, and was one of the few people to remain in her house through the amazing floods in 1960 which caused almost everyone else to evacuate the centre of Droitwich.

On this particular day I walked up the High Street to purchase one of the amazing pork rolls for which Droitwich is famous. You go into the little shop about half way along on the left hand side where a leg of pork is being carved on top of the counter wafting tantalising smells into the street so it is almost impossible to pass by.

Into a crisp roll, sliced longways, is poured a generous helping of hot gravy followed by a little light stuffing. On top of that is laid the lovely pork ready to melt in your mouth and the whole tasty mixture is closed within the roll. I can hardly ever wait to get to suitable spot before sinking my teeth into this wonderful treat which usually sets me up for the rest of the day.

The roll at first seems so enormous that it would require a rugby fifteen to eat it, but it is so good that it seems to slip down very easily.

This day, however, although my mouth was watering as usual, I began to feel pain in my leg and started to limp for no reason as I scurried towards the square. It got worse and worse and I had to sit down on a bench close to Machin's to eat my roll.

I limp when I am very tired, after say a round of golf, but this was a very bad limp and I had a feeling that something strange, and I hoped wonderful, was about to happen.

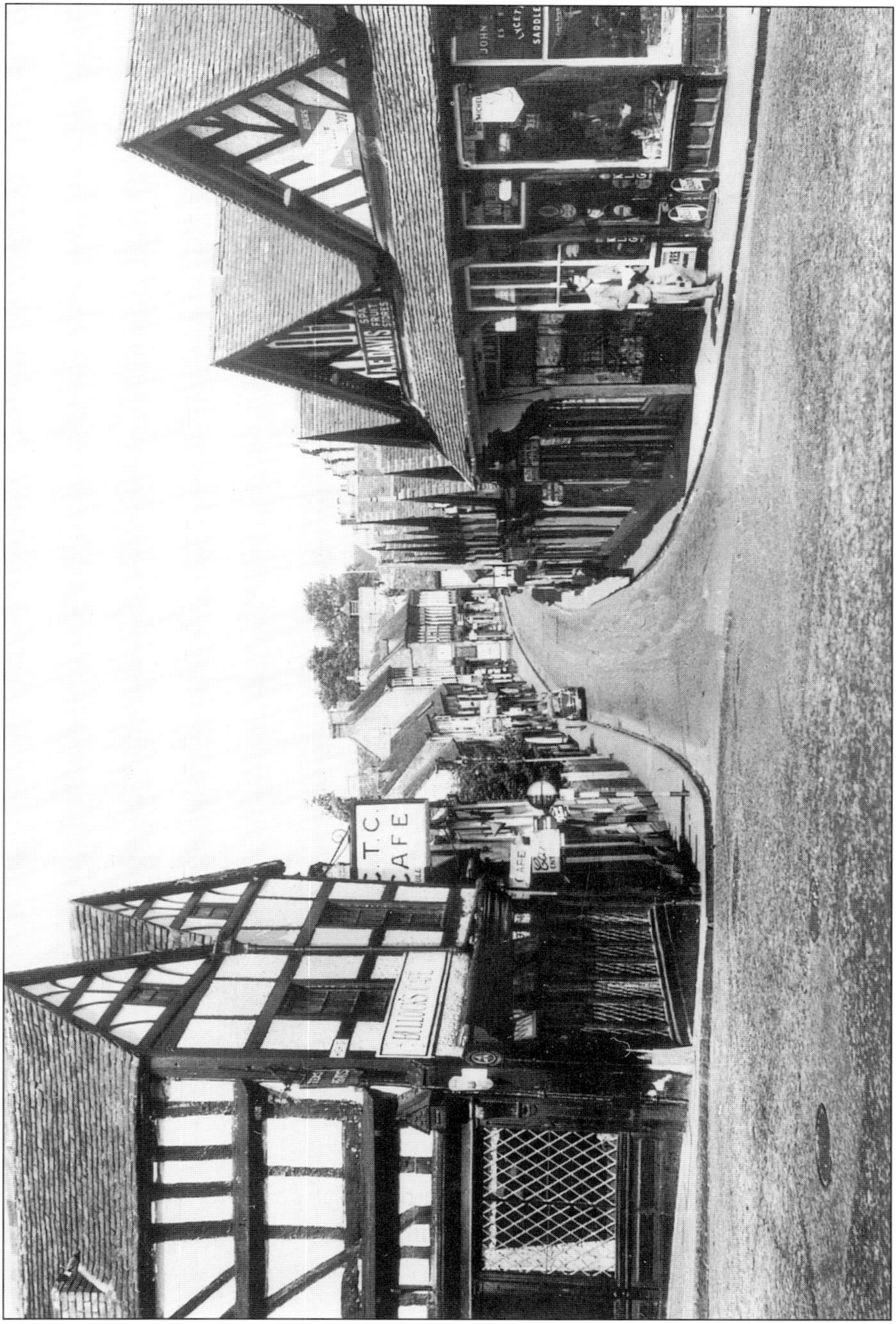
JOHN
SADDLE

I walked back to Machin's and there was Nancye waiting for me.

"There you are, you rascal" she said in her determined way,

"I have someone for you to meet - Come with me", she said, just like that, and I followed her across to her attic house tucked away in the middle of four or five other houses, almost invisible from the street, but very real when you are inside.

Nancye had once lent me a book on ghosts some time ago, and we were both agreed that the stories in the book were a bit tame "Not like the real world" she said.

"I have some people I would like you to meet" she said as we went through to her lounge for a sherry which was her tipple.

"My young cousin from Yorkshire is staying with me for a few days and she said she wanted to meet Andrew Machin's Accountant, so I have dragged you across", said Nancye.

And there, sitting as calmly as you would wish, was the young girl in a long dark dress who I had last seen in that back room in the White Lion in Haworth. Lily was radiant and as warm as ever - and when we greeted one another as long lost friends, Nancye was amazed .

"How can you possibly know Lily?" she said, "because usually she stays in Yorkshire and I only see her on very rare occasions."

"We have met from time to time, Nancye, but you mustn't tell too many people about it - we are old friends aren't we Lily?", I said.

As I was admiring Lily's dress and telling her how well she looked, Nancye said " I have lots to - make yourselves at home" - and with that spun on her heel out through the door.

As I said a rushed "thank you and goodbye" to Nancye, Lily took my arm and said "There are lots of things I want to tell you. It is only fair that you know all the story now as you really have been part of it."

"It didn't go to plan unfortunately", started Lily, "You see Elizabeth never told us she was afraid of water, and if I had only known that, I would never have let her jump. She planned to marry Captain Bidmead. How could such a thing happen?", he asked.

"The first thing that went wrong was the delay because, you remember, we couldn't get the balloon to go up on the Saturday because the weather was awful. We had to wait till the Sunday evening and that caused great difficulties because Charles had already arranged a carriage to take the happy couple away up to Scotland for their honeymoon."

"Charles and I actually watched the balloon go up from Tower Farm, Hollins Lane, Keighley, probably the highest point around. Charles knows the owners very well, and we saw quite clearly the balloon was over Ponden, but I don't think the Captain could see from where he was."

"Then, of course, when Elizabeth took off she had never told anyone of her terrible fear of water and when it seemed that she would possibly land on Ponden Reservoir, she panicked, and yes she did jump early, but only because she misjudged the height she was above the water. It is very deceptive as the water seems much closer than it actually is".

"Tragically she was injured and when the others arrived it was obvious it was a very serious injury and the plan couldn't go ahead.

"But then we realised that we had no choice - if we told people it wasn't me then we could not elope so we had to say nothing. We weren't at the landing site because we were miles away as planned, and of course the people who found her didn't know either Elizabeth or Lily and didn't consider for one moment that the poor dead girl was anyone other than Lily Cove.

Elizabeth was later buried in Haworth cemetery. People were surprised that my father didn't attend the funeral but we understand why now. We went off to be married but unfortunately could never return to Haworth for obvious reasons.

Lily continued, "Absolute secrecy was required now more so than ever - and I stayed at the Gamekeeper's coach house that I showed you, and I waited for Charles to come and pick me up. I had to change into white clothes as my disguise which worked well don't you think!."

"We travelled all the way down to Droitwich which we chose because of the wonderful Spa there . The waters worked wonders on Charles's bad back," said Lily, "and of course the business has done quite well wouldn't you say!"

"We lived, you see, with the Machin's in 11 Queens Street. It was an amazing building with a big slope towards the back, and of course the pub next door always looked as if it was leaning against our house!."

"We had to leave only when it was knocked down in 1988 - because we were disturbed . We had to move because the building was no longer there." said Lily. "We were however ever so happy and had a daughter who we called Nancye."

"It was only when you told Andrew Machin one day that you were going up to Yorkshire that I realised that we could go with you, and have a chance to make amends and tell the people what really happened", said Lily

She went on, "We lived in Droitwich to a happy old age and I knew that Charles would arrange for me to be buried in Haworth and he arranged that to be done secretly in winter. The grass in front of the grave would never grow the same as the rest would it? You noticed that I know! But it is all right now. Did you realise that there were two people in the grave?"

"The people doing the grave had to move the stone to get below it because of the slope and when they finished they unfortunately didn't put it back again. I had to have that put back otherwise it would have been awful."

"So we enlisted your help!", said Lily

"I am glad you did, and I am glad I was able to help," I said.

"So, Mr Burns, you must tell the people of Haworth what happened that day", instructed Lily.

"I will - I promise I will," I said and that is the reason I have written this book.

29.
Wrapping it up

I know that Lily is happy now and she is at peace. Her life should not have been cut short so cruelly through no fault of hers, and I know she would have wanted to have given so much to this world.

Maybe she will contact me again if she needs something. Maybe the time will come when I have a chance to contact her again. Whatever, I most certainly will respond.

I feel in my own small way I have made life happier for her and Sir Walter Scott, Cedric and Cecil, of course my great love, Mary Queen of Scots.

Are there more twists to come? I don't know.

Maybe someone out there knows the answers.

If they do . . .

ANB Started 26/12/98